PRAISE FOR
Not Even Dark Chocolate Can Fix This Mess

"A sense of humor isn't a mandatory skill in nursing…but it sure helps! Kathy Eliscu's book perfectly captures the whirl-a-minute, non-stop thinking that occupies the minds of nurses everywhere. Whether you're a nurse or just someone juggling multiple—and often competing—priorities, you'll identify with Eliscu's Tink and her crazy, stream-of-conscious thinking about work, family, life, and chocolate."

—LYN A.E. McCAFFERTY, Editor, *ADVANCE for Nurses* (2001–2010)

"*Not Even Dark Chocolate Can Fix This Mess* is a non-stop tilt-a-whirl of relationships and beastly hormones, as 54-year-old Katrinka self-medicates with chocolate. You'll see. One day your body changes, and everything spins out from there. Author Kathy Eliscu creates a comical loop-the-loop toward mindful calm."

—SUZETTE MARTINEZ STANDRING, syndicated columnist and author of *The Art of Opinion Writing* and *The Art of Column Writing*

"Kathy Eliscu always had a way with exclamation marks, and there are lots of those in *Not Even Dark Chocolate Can Fix This Mess*!! Tink is both touching and hilarious, and you will wish she were your bff!!!!!!"

— JANE P. LORD, executive editor of Maine-based *Current Publishing* and milk chocolate diehard

"Answering machine messages were never this funny. My message to you is: Read *Not Even Dark Chocolate Can Fix This Mess*. Kathy Eliscu's first book is quirky, endearing, and wonderful. I think I'll call Kathy to tell her how much I loved it."

—JERRY ZEZIMA, Stamford Advocate humor columnist and author of *Leave It to Boomer* and *The Empty Nest Chronicles*

Not even dark chocolate can fix this MESS

by **Kathy Eliscu**

illustrations by
William D. Eldridge

OK.

Deep breath.

Positive thoughts.

AAAAAAAAAAAAAARrrrrrrrRRR
RrrrrrRRRRRGG
GGGHHHH!!!
!!!!!!!!!!!!!!!!!!!!!!!!
!!!!!!!!!!!!!!!!!!!!!!!!
!!!!!!!!!!!!!!!!!!!!!!!!
!!!!!!!!!!!!!!!!!!!!!!!!
!!!!!!!!!!!!!!!!!!!!!!!!
!!!!!!!!!!!!!!!!!!!!!!!!
!!!!!!!!!!!!!!!!!!!!!!!!

AAARRGGGGHH!!

!!!!!!!!!!!!!!!!!!!!
!!!!!!!!!!!!!!!!!!!
!!!!!!!!!!!!!!!!!!!
!!!!!!!!!!!!!!!!!!!
!!!!!!!!!!!!!!!!!!
!!!!!!!!!!!!!!!!!!!
!!!!!!!!!!!!!!!!!!
!!!!!!!!!!!!!!!!!!!!

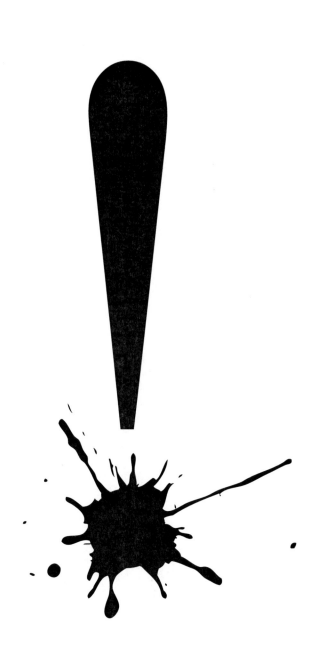

• • •

Ugh.

Well, then. That wasn't quite as loving as I'd like.

Let's start again.

• • •

And now, let us begin our story in earnest. It is the tale of a modern-day, hardworking, affable woman named Katrinka.

Katrinka has been happily serving the needs of others for many years and is soon to discover that the timing of events and her middle-aging body may have a slight effect on her longstanding pleasant nature. In spite of this, we shall keep in mind that she is, at heart, a woman of budding spiritual faith and a true and enthusiastic princess of sorts, or at least a queen or duchess. And as such, we shall all look forward, ultimately, to a happy ending, in spite of any torment encountered along the way.

Prologue

Please turn these pages very gently. I just had a two-hour nervous breakdown. My PMS dropped the P, and although I'm feeling better and have made the proper restitution with both my fiancé and the hinges on one of our kitchen drawers, I am still a little touchy. You would be, too, if on top of the hormones, your new GYN told you to cut back on the caffeine.

Choosing a new doctor is so personal. At first, everything seemed fine. I sat in the Southern Maine Women's Wonderland OB-GYN Mart waiting room for an hour—a large, busy room, a la upscale bus station, filled with women half my age, some very pregnant, others toting softly pudgy-faced, sleeping infants in carriers—until a brown-haired, expressionless, overweight 20-year-old in a pink two-piece uniform stood at the far end of the room bellowing, "Katrinka? Katrinka?" scanning back and forth with her dulled eyes. She was on her third "Katri—" when I managed to lift myself up from my stupor and barely cushioned institutional waiting room chair and she stopped paging me. I gave her a slight wave of acknowledgment, and she spun around, my signal to follow her into a small office, where I waited for the nurse to ask me all the questions I'd already answered online, on-phone, and on-paper. At least this new nurse, entering her mini-office, smiled. Once. No introduction. After another round of questioning— "When was your last period?" (I'm thinking, *Why don't you look at all the paperwork I just filled out?*)—I was brought into the exam room, given the usual quick instructions about what to leave on and what to take off and all about which way to wear the paper gown, and told that the doctor would be "right in." Eighteen minutes (or days) later—I can't remember—he entered the room with but a moment of introduction.

By now I was all sweaty from being cold in that stupid paper cloth—I don't know why they always make me sweat—and the exam began. By now, I was not feeling particularly cheery or fresh, if you know what I mean, and I was becoming a little testy and anxious.

The new gynecologist was/still is male, and seemed kind enough and listened to the high points of my medical history, which sounded something like "…two kids…natural childbirth…blah blah…period… cervix…blah blah…sore boobs…blah blah…"—you know, the usual stuff. I told him I was currently PMS-ing. But as the exam progressed, in some sick "medical" way, he started talking about my breasts and caffeine. I think you get the picture. *I'm sore*, he's poking and prodding my chest, and I'm about to have my PERIOD!!! Hel-*lo*!!! And he's telling me to reduce coffee and chocolate. Frankly, I don't know why I didn't get up and leave. Right then. Other than the fact that, save for the thin, crinkly paper gown, I was basically naked and in the stirrups and all.

I understand the link between caffeine and fibrocystic breasts and discomfort, but COME ON. *Nobody* comes between me and my coffee and chocolate, I mean NOBODY. Not even GOD ALMIGHTY would do that. I mean, God actually invented the coffee and cocoa bean, didn't She? And please, don't send me all the Internet links that say caffeine is The Devil. I DON'T CARE. You want to know what evil is? The guy who invented decaf. And the nut who thought up carob.

Why would this doctor suggest something so horrible?

Then he talked about perimenopause, a bullshit medical term referring to the time around the change of life when you want to strangle people—or hug them—due to hormones. There could be weight gain. Hot flashes. And other unpleasant-sounding symptoms. He said I might be a little scattered or forgetful. And that my mood and temper might be a bit affected.

The jerk. Clearly he does not understand women.

And I told him that on my next birthday—my 55th—I'm

planning on having my fiancé, Ben, give me a big surprise party with a gourmet chocolate mousse mocha cake and enough coffee to keep me and the entire city awake for a week, and just what did he think about that? He had the balls to say nothing. Just smiled, gave a little nod and wrote something in my chart. What a prick.

I will give him this much: his office has a spectacular rest room. That is very important to me. A pink box of Kleenex, colorful hooks on the back of the door, and the *foamy* soap—ocean breeze scent, nice and light. Very princessy. And the rest room was clean as a whistle.

~ ~ ~ ~ ~ ~ ~ ~

Groceries in arms, I put my pocketbook down on the mail-strewn kitchen table. Obviously, Ben's here somewhere, probably tinkering in the garage with his latest garden equipment project. I scan the room, a lovely sprawling farmhouse kitchen, complete with the stale odor of dirty dishes from last night and this morning, and the faint smell of dog mixed in.

I go upstairs to my office area to check for phone messages. There's a cheery receptionist from the GYN's office calling (wow—at least something about that place is fast) to see if I want to be "squeezed in tomorrow—giggle, giggle" for my annual mammogram.

Yeah, that would sure be comfy.

I HAVE PMS, AND WHAT DO THEY NOT UNDERSTAND ABOUT THAT?!

Oh, yeah—here's another thing the new doctor said:

"You're fifty-four. You should stop your periods in a year."

Just how powerful does he think I am?

Me: Well, my periods may not stop in a year. My mother went until she was—

He: Something wrong there.

Me: And my grandmother—

He: That's a problem. If you're still at it in a year, we'll do a test. Take a little sample of your uterus.

Fair enough. And if you still have a penis in a year, we'll start snipping.

I hear Ben's voice from the bottom of the stairs.

"Hey, sweetheart! Wanna go grab some dinner somewhere? I'm starving!"

"Just a minute, honey! I'm typing."

~ ~ ~ ~ ~ ~ ~ ~

The sad facts are that my former GYN became ill and had to close his practice. Um…I'm pretty sure I had nothing to do with it. I mean, my moods weren't all that assaultive. I really loved him. Going there once a year or so was like seeing an old friend that I could joke around with. Comforting, with his nice, small waiting room, years later carrying the same sweet parent and infant posters I had seen when I was pregnant two decades earlier. Same office staff. His wonderful nurse would give me my annual hug, and in return, I'd let her prick my finger. (Why does that little finger stick hurt so much?) The old "Hang in there!" poster of a cat was still taped on the ceiling above the exam table…and this man was able to gently humor me when I asked my yearly neurotic question: "So, all those instruments—they're all clean and sterile and stuff, right?"

"Meg!" he'd yell out the exam room door. "Wanna see if there's a clean speculum somewhere?"

But I'd tease him back. Afterwards, sitting in his modest-sized office, which hadn't been renovated since WW II except for updated pictures of his wife and children, frames shiny, dollar-store frugal— and now grandchildren—he'd remind me, as he did every year, to do a monthly breast exam. And he'd quiz me to see if I knew how much calcium a woman my age needed.

"Breasts monthly…Breasts monthly…Breasts monthly…" I'd chant, rocking back and forth. "But calcium? CALCIUM?!? SHUT. UP. Look at me. I missed out on the tall, thin cover-girl genes. I'm dark and European. And I'LL NEVER GET OSTEOPOROSIS." (Deep breath.) "I don't remember how much calcium."

Great guy. He'd walk me out of his office, an arm around my shoulder, and he'd mutter something about seeing me in a year.

Never once mentioned snipping my innards.

"Sweetheart?!?"

~ ~ ~ ~ ~ ~ ~ ~

Just how long can one very devoted and hungry man stand at the bottom of our staircase?!?

Look for another GYN—?

♀

Foreword

I'm an avid reader. And I didn't set out to write. I got dragged into doing it. But once I got started, it had a certain appeal. Oddly, what I wrote seemed to have had the unexpected side effect of occasionally helping others. (More later.)

See, one can be nice for just so many hours of the day, then it gets old. I'm a nurse and basically a nice person. But lately, at work, I only have a total of about an hour and a half of niceness in me. Two hours, tops. It wasn't always this way. The health-care profession has turned into a corporate monster, making it almost impossible to give, well, *care* to patients. I miss that. It's frustrating, with its endless regulations that seem to be the result of very well-paid people who have too much time on their hands. So eventually, nastiness sets into my work day, followed by consumption of large amounts of chocolate.

Oh. About reading.

My biggest complaint about some books is that by the fourth page, you've been introduced to 47 characters. I'm 54. I can barely remember my own name and what I'm doing half the ~~broccoli decaf tea paper towels toilet paper protein bars~~…oh. Sorry.

So here is a list of main characters to which you can refer back as needed.

Note to my high school English teachers: I hope you realize that my participle did not dangle in the previous sentence. Proper use of language is very important to Aunt Tink. Unless angry, in which case it's perfectly acceptable to curse like a sailor.

If you think this is one of those books that flows or has a concept or vision or even a plan of some sort, I really apologize. I just can't seem to stick with one thing. My middle-aged brain is like my house. There are little piles of stuff here and there. Ben and I always talk about organizing. Sometimes on weekends, we actually start doing that. Often, when I'm going through the first pile of mail, newspapers, and candy wrappers on the kitchen table and separating them out, Ben will walk into the room and ask, "Wanna go get coffee and drive to the flower place?"

Iced café mocha? Our favorite nursery? Gorgeous plants and a visit to their gift shop? While we are finally trying to clean up?!?

OK.

Then we buckle up and I pull out my Starbucks card extra fast. If you have the energy to follow this story, I promise it will take you nowhere. You will have learned nothing, and you and I will both still have piles of crap lying around.

{ *MAIN CHARACTERS* }

Aunt Tink/Aunt T/ Tink (me, Katrinka Casawill)—age 54, several people's ex-wife, mother of two (Ali and Dylan, listed below), grandmother of two as of this writing, Ben's fiancée, various people's aunt, sister, cousin, daughter…well, it's a big family…a nurse at a big hospital clinic in Maine, and now a part-time advice columnist ("Ask Aunt Tink")! And weirdly, an Associate of The Sisters of Our Most Precious Lord. I love this group of good Sisters and lay persons—and I have great intentions as an Associate, but I routinely miss almost every meeting. Except the annual Christmas party.

My life has recently taken some difficult turns, but I never thought it would get to the point of needing to—well, let's move along for now.

The main thing to remember about me is that if you agree with me on anything (simply by making eye contact and stating a sincere "I agree"), then we'll be friends and hang out at my favorite place together—Starbucks.

Ben Lambert—my fiancé. We met at work and fell in love. He was the first man I laughed with to the point of asthma. Our friendship grew into a playful flirtation and eventually into a deep and abiding love. OK, wait. We were crazy, like a couple of teenagers. He's older than ~~me I~~ me. (Shut up, Miss Nesbaum, 11th grade English.) A lot older. How sexy is that?! And I can't believe I'm giving him second billing. However, in the six years I've known him, he's earned it by being a great father type to my grown kids and by saying things to me like: "I love your body! It's luscious and soft!" That, in case you are a male reading this, is the exact fabulous thing to say to a woman in her middle years. Our relationship is close, yet we're independent. We even have separate land lines in our house. Ben and I have an unspoken loyalty, and occasionally talk about making our union "official." Our past wild days—the 1960s—are behind us, thank God. Although he can still be seen on a quiet Saturday night, staring off into space sitting in the living room and holding the Gibson guitar an old girlfriend gave him in 1969 as a break-up gift. Antiwar protests, free love, and a guitar he never really learned to play.

Ben and I have a nice life together, and do fun things like going out for coffee or breakfast on the weekends. His kisses are soft and taste like pistachio nuts. Love that. After I fell for him, that first kiss sealed the deal. I can tell you about it because he will probably never read this. Oh, he'll pretend, but he'll just skim it—fine with me, and I won't have to explain the pistachio nut thing. The one complaint I have about Ben is that he has been known to eat fabulous pastries in front of me without offering to share until I practically beg or bribe. "I'm saving you from yourself," he says, buttery crumbs dropping all over his lap. Serves me right for always talking up a diet I'm never really on. Oh—and this I'll-eat-anything-I-want-regardless-of-fat-and-sugar-content guy? He's a man of science. And trim.

Little Tink/Little T/LT—my wonderful niece, age 30, who sings, dances, acts, plays piano, and somehow remains sweet and kind in spite of being in show biz. Her parents, both "lifers" in the military, have been stationed about a bazillion miles from here, somewhere in Asia, since she finished college. She's my oldest brother's only child, so I keep a close relationship with her. It is this brilliant woman who inadvertently almost drove me to a nervous collapse this year. (Again, more later.) She is also my coffee soul mate. We discovered this when she was visiting nearby last year.

"I'm so down…" she'd sighed to me.

I studied her sweet, fair-skinned face, her sad, clear-blue eyes, her wispy auburn curls falling down from her hair clip. "Let's go get a coffee and talk," I suggested in a loving aunt-y sort of way. I figured she was distressed about not having a special someone with whom to share her life. Ten minutes later, at you-know-where (Starbucks: see previous part about you and me being good friends), she was laughing, chatting away… well, actually, she was tap dancing on the little round wood table, cleverly avoiding my iced latte, re-clipping her hair every few minutes. So it turns out that her "special someone" is contained in a twelve-ounce cardboard cup and that she'd been given decaf, not real coffee, where she'd been staying. Her hostess had misread the coffee container label. Some people! Well, actually, it was my mom, who hadn't fully understood the concept of putting one's eyeglasses upon one's face until this little incident.

Ali—my grown daughter, who is beyond cute and smart. She's dark, like me, but without the occasional wispy gray hair, and she's taught me things like how to get the stains out of white clothes with some handheld bleach-y thing. Once I may have overdone her method a little on my favorite white sweater. OK, I rubbed the living hell out of it twice daily for two weeks.

"Oh?" she asked. "Did it make a hole? Sometimes that happens."

It was hard to be annoyed with her. When she smiles, she has such an adorable dimple. So, all in all, between her household advice, which I no longer use, and her dimple, I think I actually deserved a new white sweater.

Hope you followed that.

She's a good mom to her kids and always finds those teachable moments. Like when she's driving them to school, she quizzes them on their spelling words. ("Holy crap! We're so late! Katie, please spell tardiness. T-a-r-d-i—")

Ali lends me good books to read and doesn't get pissed off at me when I gently suggest that she and her kids might be a little less stressed without soccer practice and tap dance lessons for young children. And piano and Suzuki violin and gymnastics. And Science camp. And Church camp. And Play Group. And…

Ali—and now her family—are also vegan. She spends hours coming up with exciting, nutritious dishes that I'm really glad I don't have to eat.

She's such a wonderful and involved mother that I wish she could come be my mother and help me out. Despite the occasional health or household hints and mundane advice I give my "Ask Aunt Tink" readers, my place is a mess and my life has become, well…we'll talk.

John—Ali's husband, who is a doctor. Do you hear me? A *DOCTOR*. Enough said. Well, OK. He's handsome and likes the Simpsons and is very nice to me in spite of everything I've ever done, or not done, as his mother-in-law. He and Ali and their children—my adorable grandkids—live about a thousand miles away, but we talk on the phone. And I recently got one of those video cams so we can see each other between visits. After trying it and accidentally hanging up on them roughly fifty times, I figured it out, so that thing about old dogs learning new tricks is just dead wrong. Just don't ask me about using an iPod—ever. Or anything else new and electronic that involves, like, five remotes for the same mountain of machinery with buttons and dials.

…Deep breath…
"Tink! Dinner! Wanna get going?!?"
Oops! *Ben.*
"*Sorry*, Ben. Be right down. Let's just get something light tonight, OK?"
Damn diet.

Katie—my granddaughter, the greatest artist or gymnast of our time. I'll keep you posted. Now age seven. Like her mommy, she has that Italian skin, shining dark eyes, and soft black hair. And cute as a button.

Elliott—my grandson. Plays a mean violin since age two and gives really yummy hugs. He's three. He still smells fresh and baby-new, especially under his chin. I know that from when I catch him long enough for a hug and kiss. Looks like a miniature of his dad, John—light brown hair, blue-green eyes, sturdy but not overweight. Little Man material.

Ring. Ring. Beep. "Hi. It's Tink. Leave a message."

"Tink? Tink?!? It's Dad. Dad. Over at—oh, where am I now? You know. Well anyway, the phone rang a few minutes ago and I was—oh, where was I?—you know, in the, uh, *rest*room, and I heard it ringing and ringing and when I came out it wasn't ringing and I don't know who—well, was it you, Tink? Did you call me? Tink? Are you there? Oh, darn it, I guess you're—well, call me as soon as you get this, will you? It's Dad. Dad. Your father. Uh, well…" (*Click.*)

Ah…my dad. Tell you about him in a minute.

Dylan—my youngest—in college, out of state—a bright and talented student, who, in his most honest moments, has wondered if he could make a living "sitting on my ass." Frankly, I think he could. He's a very sweet kid who at eleven was chubby and is now tall, dark, and yes, handsome, and always has a nice girlfriend. And he loves his mommy—me—a lot. I make him say that part when he's home. I have pictures of him all over the house of the school plays he was in and sports he played in high school…and middle school…grammar school…church school…

Marge—aka "**Gaga**"—my mother…my dear, precious mother, who passed away several months ago, but is still the pivotal force in our family. And although an outstanding and respected college professor, her most impressive moments, in my opinion, were avoiding her physical therapy sessions in the last weeks of her life by pressuring us into taking her to the parking lot of her favorite dress shop instead.

She would sit in the car while saleswomen, to her utter delight, hustled clothing out to the car. Think I'm kidding? I have the sales slips and the credit card bills to prove it. Almost a year later, I still get offers for her from various department stores. I'm a little pissed off at her for dying. Not that she wanted to. I miss her terribly. She was the kind of warm and dynamic mom other kids wished they had. I mean, she would take me out of school to go to a Broadway show and out to lunch. Now I have inherited my dad. I adore him, but he just doesn't cut it as a lady.

Martin—aka "**Hipa**"—my dad. Poor guy. Married to my mom for sixty-something years before she died. I don't say "poor guy" because he was married to her. No, he was crazy about her, and she him. In fact, no matter what the words or deed, the other admired it.

"Martin," she'd say, "I'm afraid I had a mishap with the car today. Totaled it."

"Isn't she wonderful?" he'd ask me, eyes shining.

Of course, he's partly deaf. No; I say "poor Dad" because he's alone now. Sort of. He lives in an assisted living place nearby and spends his days with about twenty other men and roughly three thousand "senior" females. That's how the numbers generally work post-eighty. So he spends a lot of time ducking stylish old ladies calling after him, "Martin! Oh, hi, Martin!"

"Tink! Should I just bring in some take-out?"
"I'M COMING!!!"

So, to continue… "TIIINNNKKKKK!!!!!"
Jeez…

~ ~ ~ ~ ~ ~ ~ ~

Jody's Grille House

2 Cobb salad, fat-free dsg @8.95 ea. 17.90 *350 calories*

1 Perrier w/lemon 2.25 2.25 *0 cal!*

1 Diet Pepsi 1.95 1.95 *0 cal!!*

2 Coffee—black @2.00 ea. 4.00 *0!!!!!!*

1 Ultimate Mocha Mountain 7.95 7.95 *uh...150+75+*

1 Str.-rhub. a la mode 5.95 5.95 *...oh fuck!*

Subtotal 40.00

Tax 2.40

Total 42.40

Thanks!

Jessica

I feel fat.

Remember—keep sm. piece drk. choc. in purse-
Assoc. that w/inner peace feeling? Practice.

Apparently Still the Foreword

Richard—my brother, age 51. Lives an hour away. We dubbed him Saint Richard due to all the caretaking he did for my parents in the last few years. I'm talking countless visits to doctors, helping with errands, all that goes into helping folks that get old and ill, and he did it with patience. He developed the fine art of sitting and waiting, and standing and waiting, and waiting and waiting, and only griped to me occasionally. He's a schoolteacher and gets summers off. Great guy, needs another wife. Wait. Wait! He needs *a* wife. He's been divorced for years and shares custody of his kids, very nicely parenting them, I might add. Not that I'm matchmaking. A *music* teacher, still has lots of thick dark hair at his age, and maybe needs to lose a few pounds. OK, 30. But what a sweetie! Again, not that I'm matchmaking. He volunteers in a music project for special ed teens, and you should see how gentle and lovely he is with those kids. NOT THAT I'M MATCHMAKING.

OK, once in a while I try to pair up a couple of people I know who I think could use a little company.

Let me further say that I have a 100%—100%!—failure rate.

"Stop trying to matchmake!" Ben hollers at me at least once a week.

"OK," I lie, "I will. I'm done. No more."

I wait 'til he's out of the room to pick up the phone or send off the next e-mail.

"I think I'll just look up my bank statement online," I call after him. Then I begin typing.

"Jenny, hi! Remember me from our book club? Wondered if you're still single. My brother…"

But anyway. The only thing about my brother is that he sometimes acts a little lame about the whole dating thing. And he doesn't always know social protocol. Which is why he needs my help. Example: When Ben and I were making plans to celebrate our first New Year's Eve together, he showed up at our house at, like, 11 p.m. "I was in the area!" he smiled. "Thought I'd stop by and bring in the New Year with you guys!" I was not happy and started to gently kick him out, but Ben, who had hit it off with Richard right from the start, invited him in, and they sat in front of the TV, doing a running commentary on some big holiday music special. That sure was romantic.

So—my brother's phone number is 603-76?-??. It really is. I mean, what good would it do to give out one of those fake numbers like they use on *Law and Order*: 555-0100? Everyone knows they're bogus. OK, I guess to protect his confidentiality, I'll give this number instead: 1-555-555-555-555-603-76?-??. Please, no weirdos.

Back to the character list:

Note to Self: Hurry up already with the damn character list!

Note to Self: SHUT. UP.

"**Tink!** Are you coming to bed anytime soon?"

"Just a minute, sweetie!"

> One time I approached a new friend who is an absolute sweetheart of a guy.
>
> "Mitch," I said, "do you date?"
>
> He looked at me. For a minute I think he thought I was making a play for him, even though he knows that Ben and I are a tight couple.
>
> He smiled and said, "Tink—I'm gay!"
>
> "Great!" I yelled.
>
> See, I thought so, so I had a name in each pocket of my matchmaking apron. I arranged a casual meeting with a gay male friend of mine at a party. I guess sparks did not fly.
>
> I told you. 100% failure rate.

Sincere Apologies—
More Foreword

Lorraine—my cousin, who was very close to my mother, on account of her own mother being less than optimal at the nurturing thing. She was at our house in NY so much growing up, she's like my little sister. She moved to Pittsburgh after college, then my folks moved to Maine, but Lorraine keeps in close contact with everyone. She's a single mom with a 10-year-old daughter. Lorraine is 45, looks 35, complains like she's 15. I wouldn't even try to match her up with anyone. Too picky. But brilliant and beautiful. A gifted artist whose work crosses from the world of sculpture into architectural design. She'll probably be pissed I'm not putting her phone number in here. Tell you what: Call my brother Richard. He's such a saint, he'll screen the calls for her.

Father Rob—When I need reassurance or a kind voice to bounce things off of, I turn to Fr. Rob. He was the first priest I really knew. WAIT. I don't mean that in the biblical sense. Even though he is adorable and a few years younger than me. OK, maybe a decade. And a half. And looks like a movie star. Ugh. Go figure. But anyway. I met him when I was joining the Catholic Church about fifteen years ago. He lives out of state now, but was our parish priest back then and is an absolute sweetheart of a guy. Very accepting. Didn't mind that I was fourteen different religions before converting. I like to see all angles before I decide.

Phew! That's the end of the main character list, though there will be brief appearances by my dog in the role of Lounger, Eater, and Sniffer. Minor characters will show up now and then. I can't help that.

My work friend Nellie (oh—I forgot to list her) says that around this age people can get a little scattered. At least she didn't mention the caffeine or mood thing. She knows better.

You can write minor characters in at the end of the chapter. You know, the various Sisters, the mailman, the—

What? Do I have to do *everything*?!? See, that's what's wrong with you people!

Oh.

Sorry.

TO RECAP:

Tink (me)—Always right. Loves Starbucks.

Ben—Says the right things. Loves Starbucks but taunts me with cheese Danish.

Little Tink—Broadway material; desperately needs daily Starbucks.

Ali—Like a beauty queen, but ethical. Knows her stain removers. Vegan. Starbucks, hold the cream. That's "c-r-e-a-"

"Tink? Are you coming to bed, honey dear?"

Ugh. Eleven p.m. already? Remembering I'd just recently promised myself I'd get more rest…

John—Doctor. Nine out of ten recommend coffee. Starbucks.

Katie and Elliott—Grandchildren. Never too young for Starbucks. No caffeine.

Dylan—Successful sitting-on-his-ass executive material. Will probably own Starbucks someday.

Marge—Deceased. Socialized anywhere, including Starbucks.

Martin—Aging. Probably doesn't remember me taking him to Starbucks.

Richard—603-76/-5/

Lorraine—Call Richard.

Fr. Rob—Can priests drink coffee?

Major workplace characters:

Dr. Ernie Myers—my boss. Such a corporate robot we don't even know if he has a digestive system, much less drinks coffee. Looks like—well—like nothing. He actually looks like nothing. Amazingly nondescript, quiet with even speech. Maybe he really is a robot.

Dr. D.—a young, whiney doctor on my "team" whose job it is to drive me crazy. Whitish-blonde and skinny, a frequent user of eucalyptus cough drops, even though I have never known him to cough or be ill, ever.

Gloria—my 40-ish, petite, strawberry blonde nursing supervisor who drinks coffee or wine or whatever is available in order to cope with Dr. D. and the whole dysfunctional bunch. She buys expensive clothes and goes on vacations A LOT. Hey—we all have to cope. I just don't think it's fair, or even nice, for people to be their teenage weight, and that's why I have to smack her someday.

Peggy—my office mate, a true and steady nurse.

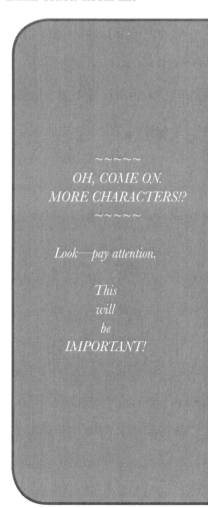

OH, COME ON.
MORE CHARACTERS!?

Look—pay attention.

This
will
be
IMPORTANT!

Those are the main work folks—a great bunch—really, just great. Yeah. Really. Absolutely.

Stay tuned for more of this crew of misfits, of which I am a member.

Oh, yeah—**and a bunch of nuns**. And **some other people**. I don't remember who. Just some others, OK?

I have got to get some sleep.

√ out bks. on good health & stuff. food—

exer.—etc.

From the desk of Ben,

to anyone disturbed enough to read this:

Good luck. Get up frequently for snacks.
You're gonna need them.
It's like an alien abduction...

EXTRA CHARACTERS (write small) if you're still reading this:

_____

_____

_____

_____

_____

I know. I didn't think you'd do this either.

{ CHAPTER 1 }

In which our hero is thrown into a whirlwind of external and internal pressures... aka Thank-God-I-Thought-We'd-Never-Get-Here.

My parents appointed me power of attorney a couple of years ago. They apparently trusted me. This trust was, also apparently, so deep and abiding that they did not feel a need to let me know, verbally, in writing, in mime, or in any other way, what their wishes were. About anything. Which is just weird, for two reasons. First, because we were very close. Second, because I was too numb to ask. I guess none of us could bear to talk about it. And I thought we were a fairly evolved batch. It's been a nightmare of a scavenger hunt to sort my folks' business matters and the contents of their condo. Everything eventually ended up being shoved into the two biggest storage units available in the state of Maine. I figure the whole family will sort through this stuff. They have to. I mean, my mom can't help it that she's in heaven, and my dad isn't much help, either. His brain is not at its peak functioning. When I ask him about any of it, he gives his award-winning smile, shrugs his shoulders, and says, "I don't know." If you ever want to get back at someone, appoint that person your power of attorney and tell them nothing. It took months just to find all Mom's credit cards to cancel them, and I usually end up doing these and other business tasks after a full workday, when I'm already bushed. My mother was on more mailing lists than I can count, only now the stuff arrives at *my* address, since I'm the personal representative.

And I always thought my parents liked me.

~ ~ ~ ~ ~ ~ ~ ~

MARGE CASAWILL!
~ANNOUNCING THE NEW COSMETICS LINE~

A NEW WAVE IN
ANTI-AGING PROTECTION!

CALL TODAY TO ORDER!
1-800-

Sigh.

I pick up the phone and dial.

Ring. Ring. Ri—

"Thank you for calling Bl—"

"Customer Service, please!"

"How may I direct your call, ma'am?"

"To someone in charge of your mailing list."

"You'll have to be more specific, ma'am."

"OK. You sent a letter to my mother asking her if she wants to try a new anti-aging formula. And stop calling me ma'am."

"I'm so sorry, ma'a— um, to whom am I speaking?"

"To the daughter of Marge Casawill, to whom this mailing was sent."

"And did you want to order the product for her?"

I pause.

"Actually? Yes. But only if it can be shipped."

"Well, we can ship virtually anywhere, m—, um, miss, uh…"

"Anywhere?"

"Yes, anywhere. Free of charge."

"OK, I'll order a bottle."

"And where would you like it shipped?"

"To HEAVEN, you *moron!*"

Click!

I guess that may have been one of my little still-have-your-period-at-54 moments.

~ ~ ~ ~ ~ ~ ~ ~

In the aftermath of my rage, I feel just…sadness. Deep sadness, missing my mom. It doesn't seem right that she's gone. And I don't know where my kindness has gone.

> **To: FrRob@StPeter.org**
> **From: Tink@maine.com**

Hello, Fr. Rob. So—you're pretty sure there's an afterlife, right? 'Cause for me, it's like a good news/bad news joke. I want to see my mother again. But basically, if there's really a heaven and a hell, I'm screwed.

Sorry. About the language.

Love,

Tink

…calm…rest…

What do I have—seven or eight new offers for Mom in the mail? Where has she stashed all her credit cards? How will I…*peace*…ever find them…*rest…*

[√] old pocktbks. in boxes "bedrm stuff"

{ CHAPTER 2 }

Katrinka reflects upon her mother and her own femaleness...

Being a woman isn't easy. But we spend a lot of time making it look easy. That's where the barrelful of cosmetics and personal care products and electronic devices comes in. But add in a job. Children. Aging parents. Social conscience. Food choices. Friends. Organic versus Who-Gives-A-Shit-It-Just-Tastes-Good. Spirituality. Iced café mochas. The complexities are enough to make my head spin, a very scary sight about which movies have been made.

Ring. Ring. Beep. "Hi. It's Tink. Leave a message."

"Hi, Aunt Tink! It's Little Tink. Calling 'cause I miss you. By the way, I'm really hoping to get to Maine soon. And hey—I hear the furniture from Gaga and Hipa's condo is up for grabs. Do you still have some bookshelves? Call me!" *Click.*

This is from my niece, the major talent. Oo-o-o, I love hearing from her.

Wait.

She's calling me about bookshelves? She should be out there auditioning!!!

Every. Spare. Minute.

Where was I?

Oh, yeah. Being a woman.

Give me five extra hours in the day for all of the above, plus an extra couple of dozen hours a month just to sort through the choices in the "feminine products" section of the drugstore. Which never feels all that feminine. Especially when walking down the aisle to the cash register carrying a huge box of ultra-savings-ultra-absorbent-deodorant-or-non-deodorant-wings-or-no-wings-protective-lining-cottony-soft-ultra-slim-maxi-cottony-plasticized-lined-regular-or-chlorine-free box of pads. It used to be so simple. And who invented wings? Wings?!? So the soiled pad can take flight?!? Don't tell me a woman had anything to do with that. All wings serve to do is stick to the hair, and I think you know what I'm talking about. There you are, in the middle of an important business meeting, you turn the wrong way, and you feel that familiar sharp pull. Your boss thinks you're wincing at the last idea he mentioned, and now you're being asked why you think it's a bad idea…

You may be thinking, why not tampons? Why not, indeed? They're fine, if you have a reliable watch and remember to remove them before the dreaded TOXIC SHOCK sets in. But at 54, I can't remember much of anything anymore: Is it in there? Or not? How to know…so there you are, in the middle of your workday, finding a clean bathroom (*as if*) where you can do the necessary preparations with washing hands and so on before beginning the major investigation… because, God forbid, you don't want to get TOXIC SHOCK. All this while you hear near-constant knocking on the bathroom door and know that when you open it, a half dozen of your coworkers will be in line, waiting. And looking back and forth between you and their watches.

Back in the 1960s, my mother had been at a lunch gathering of a half dozen or so women. I guess Mom was something of an adventurer in her day. One of the women at the table mentioned she had her period and what a pain it was to change her pad again. "What?" my mom asked. "Don't you use tampons?" and she pulled one out of her handbag, gave some cursory instructions to her friend, and sent her on her way to the bathroom. When the friend returned, they resumed their dessert and card game. After a short while, her friend said, "Marge, I don't know how you can stand these. They're so uncomfortable!" Turns out she'd pushed the whole thing up there, including the cardboard applicator.

Remem. to √ w/Gloria/Nellie/Peggy/other RNs @ work—re female GYN?

{ CHAPTER 3 }

The fine line between love and obligation.

ing. Ring. Beep. "Hi. It's Tink. Leave a message."

"Tink? It's your cousin Lorraine. Hey, can you send me a few of the nice teacups from your mom's collection? Any color at all. Maybe the next time you go out to the condo? I'll pay you back for mileage and mailing. What is it? About thirty miles each way? Look, there's no rush. But next week would be great! On a day when you're not working. Thanks. Uh—it's not snowing there, is it?" *Click.*

I guess I could go out there. It's just so sad to walk into my parents' condo with its cheery red-and-white kitchen dishes and fluffy light-yellow bathroom towels, some with little ducks on them, everything matching so sweetly. It brings back all the love and loss and powerful memories of the times my mom and I spent together—the laughing and silliness, the family gatherings, our frequent outings, and finally, helping her when she became so ill.

But Mom and Lorraine were close. Though it's been a long day at work and I'm tired, I get back into the car. I've got to tackle the packing again anyway, and maybe I can find some teacups for Lorraine. In the back of my mind, I think that if I go there often enough, it will help me cope with my loss. Then again, sometimes the back of my mind doesn't know shit.

Now, standing in the middle of the condo, I am surrounded by a room only half packed, a trail of tape, markers, and packing foam leading from piles to boxes and onward in a swirl of junk and treasures.

The craziness of my workplace, only an hour ago, creeps into my head as I stand in my parents' condo, looking at the disarray. Managers' talk of building renovation: new phone and computer systems, complex state regulations, a proposal for everyone to have beepers, and 24-hour availability. Holy crap. I look around the huge mess at the condo and I wonder which situation is more overwhelming. Then my eyes focus in on the unsorted stacks of business documents piled up on my mom's beautiful oak roll-top desk, the one she loved so much that she set aside money month after month to get it refinished. I realize I am packing up their lives. Flooded with emotion and fatigue, I feel the water coming into my eyes.

After a half hour of sorting, I give up and drive home. I have four beautiful teacups and saucers carefully wrapped in a box in my car.

~ ~ ~ ~ ~ ~ ~ ~

To: Tink@maine.com
From: FrRob@StPeter.org

Dear Tink,

I know. It really hurts ☹ to lose your mother. But the answer to your question is a resounding YES! There certainly is an afterlife with our Lord and those who have gone before us.

Remember that God is holding you. ☺

Always,

Fr. Rob ☺

P.S.—You know, your mother really did have a lot of nerve dying. I'm still ticked off at my mother. It's been ten years. Biggest problem was dealing with all her stuff. She never threw anything out.

```
Hope that is different in your case. Get plenty
of rest, OK? ☺
```

Well, see? It's like instant payback. I decide to do a good deed (getting the teacups for Lorraine.) And then I get Fr. Rob's reassuring, spiritual e-mail.

Maybe I should take his advice. Rest. Take a quiet walk. Try not to do too much at once.

*…time to rest…float away…peace…bills to sort through…ugh—*bills!

Ring. Ring. Beep. "Hi. It's Tink. Leave a message."

"Tink? Tink!?! It's Dad. Dad! I need you! I…I need to talk to you! Are you home?"

And I pick up the phone.

Our hero takes a break from daily tasks
to complain about public bathrooms and inhumanity.

The toilet paper brand at work is "Proclaim." *Proclaim*! Sounds important. Let's "proclaim" it to the world! Probably replaced the last brand called "Adequate." Way better than the old standard "Crumble." Think I'm kidding? Think what you like. In a restaurant bathroom, I saw a toilet paper called "Harmonious." Now *that's* something to sing about! To be one with the universe in one big peaceful pee! Why not one called "Explode"? It adds that extra excitement. Or "Mensa-Mensa"—the only paper made for women—a bit boring to look at, but boy, is it absorbent, for those special female times of the month.

I am at the movies by myself. (Yay! Chick flick!) I have a secret passion for romantic movies and love stories, but only if they have happy endings. Follow my reasoning here: If I see them enough, the good parts will rub off, right? Ben practically pushed me out the door and told me to go to a matinee. Said he'd even make supper for us later, a good deal even if he makes a mess of the kitchen and I have to go behind his back to re-clean the counters properly. Germs.

I rush to the ladies' room during the previews. The stall, constructed by a descendant of the Marquis De Sade, has a toilet paper holder approximately ten inches behind my, um, behind. There is no mechanical means of reaching it without removing my left arm. So there I am, getting up, digging into the metal cavern called a toilet paper dispenser, to find a roll that has no beginning and no end, my backside sliding and bumping up against the opposite stall wall.

Drip.

Who the hell thinks up these designs?!? Oh, yeah—and I'm holding a newly unraveled minipad between my teeth, trying not to drool on it. *Because I have my period.* And I'm mouth breathing because of the heavy scent of continuous-release bathroom fresheners.

I'm not quite as flexible as I was a couple of decades ago. Just to find the end of the roll, I have to bend forward and look up into the metal cavern, putting my head one gruesome inch and a half from the bowl itself. Not where I want my head to be. Especially because my hair's a little longer right now and it's just tucked into my collar. I hope. Now I've moved the teeth-held clean pad to the second-in-command spot, snugly held in my clothed right armpit, ignoring the mouth drool on my shirt due to the mouth breathing. Hope I don't miss the beginning of the movie. I hate that as much as seeing a movie that ends in tragedy.

After I wash my hands, I look at the no-touch sensor paper-towel dispenser on the wall, called "So Intuitive2." Not just "So Intuitive" or "So Intuitive1," which probably had to retrain itself to reach "So Intuitive2" level. Takes me a moment to figure out whether to pass my hands over the little part that looks like a bicycle reflector, or press it, so I do both, a couple of times, 'til it responds. This amazing space-age machine senses when you need a paper towel. Does it holler after women who don't wash their hands? ("You! Come back here and wash your hands! Because I said so, young lady!!") Guess they'd call that the "Nag." Or the "Mom." The "Mom 2" would also whisper "Be careful" and slip you a condom.

Recently, I was at a rest stop in the South where the toilet paper holder was locked and bolted. Yes, you read that right. It was bolted to the side of the stall so the roll could not be removed. Come on. If someone is so desperate and poor that they can't buy a roll of toilet paper, can't we just help them out? Holy shit. People are so cruel.

Oh—the movie. Yay! This is SO fun.

Do this—movie in p.m.—more oft.

{CHAPTER 5}

Katrinka discovers she is being pulled in some surprising directions.

~ ~ ~ ~ ~ ~ ~ ~ ~

~REFLECTIONS FROM THE SISTERS
OF OUR MOST PRECIOUS LORD~
DEAR SISTERS AND ASSOCIATES,
WE HAVE AN EXCITING YEAR COMING UP!
PLEASE WATCH FOR IMPORTANT
MAILINGS REGARDING OUR *JOURNEY*
INITIATIVE.
YOURS IN OUR MERCIFUL LORD,
SISTER MARY HOWARD

> *Hi, Tink! How are things? Thinking of you—still remember your mother's funeral—it was beautiful. She is surely with the Lord.*
> *Love,*
> *Sister Howard*

Oh, that's so kind of her. I slowly place the letter back on the table the same way I gently hang up the phone after a conversation in which tender words have been spoken, as though the inanimate object needed physical tenderness, having carried the softest of intentions.

Telemarketers? That's a different story.

I toss the empty envelope into the garbage. Enough with recycling every damn thing.

I know. I'll try harder.

I feel guilty and retrieve it from the top of the garbage. At least there wasn't anything gross touching it. I set it on the chair to add to the newspaper pile later, and go back to the mail pile to see—

Wait. What the—?

SPECIAL OFFER FOR
MARGE CASAWILL!
FREE HEALTHY HEARING CHECK-UP!
*Do you notice people can't always understand you?
*Do you have the feeling others aren't paying attention to you?
*Do you sometimes...

Oh, please.

I trash it angrily and go upstairs to my computer to check e-mails.

To: Tink@maine.com

From: LittleTink@NY.com

    aunt t—hate to bother you—you have a lot of
pressure at your job—but i used to call Gaga
A LOT—anyway...i'm totally discouraged about the
whole audition scene here. Chicago was easier.
but NY? i'm getting swallowed up. Gaga used to say
stuff like "hang in there"—now I feel like "hang
it up." help!
    xox LT
    ps - just text me if you're too busy

Awww, poor Little Tink... although I've put the entire Western hemisphere on notice that it'll be a cold day you-know-where-and-I-don't-mean-Maine before I'll start texting. I'm too old to learn that shit.

Ring. Ring. Beep. "Hi. It's Tink. Leave a message!"

"Tink? It's Lorraine. About your mom's teacup collection? I was thinking. I'd really like to have that blue and yellow one…" *Click.*

Huh?!?

I take a deep breath and focus on my intention to be merciful to others, something that is actually rare to think about when the pace of life has become so quick and complex that I'm in a nearly subconscious state at times. Deep down, these calls and e-mails make me feel, well, popular. If I don't think about anything too much, and continue to extend myself, there's the potential for personal reward. I like being a princess, but I especially want to be a hero. Which makes me a very good princess, in my mind. Kind of like being in a fun movie, but without the popcorn. However, none of this makes for a very good Associate of the Sisters of Our Most Precious Lord.

I do the best I can. And it gets me thinking about what I can do to help others in my life.

Little T—likes tall? short men? narrow search!
Keep to self 'til match found!

To: LittleTink@NY.com
From: Tink@maine.com

Sweetie, I am so happy to help.

It must be really hard to be an aspiring actress in New York! But *New York*?!? I mean, what drive you have! Not to mention talent. I am SO proud of you! How many people just dream and don't act on their dreams?!? A LOT, that's how many. You just stay with it, sweetheart, OK?

And meanwhile, let me give you a tip. You know, I lived in NY when I was in nursing school. Let me tell you, you learn fast to protect yourself in the city. ALWAYS LEAVE A CAR LENGTH IN FRONT OF YOU AT RED LIGHTS IN CASE SOMEONE TRIES TO GET INTO YOUR CAR. So you can go around the car in front of you if you have to.

xox Aunt T

To: LittleTink@NY.com
From: Tink@maine.com

Oh. I didn't realize you had to sell your car for voice lessons.

Love,

Aunt T

Ugh. Who am I to give advice? *Stupid* princess.

And that's when I catch myself reaching for the phone to call my mom.

Beepers; ice cream; dates; clippers.

Tuesday a.m. Work desk. Prioritize.

E-mail from Gloria, my nursing supervisor, the person I laugh with, cry on, and scream to, all at the same time. We always end up reminiscing about the olden days in nursing school, including detailed descriptions of nursing caps. Mine was the wing type, blue and maroon stripes across it, once very crisp and attractive, now kinda moldy. Hers was a pillbox kind. We talk about our kids and how they're growing up. She keeps an ample supply of Kleenex handy, for both of us. These frequent "sessions" usually end with us running together across the street to the corner store and getting soda and chips, just like we all did back in the days before something as dumb as "optimal health" came into the picture. Usually the walk back from the store becomes a mad dash, as Gloria realizes she's late for a patient or some important management meeting. Her chat gets faster and faster and she forges ahead and I try to catch up to her and her words and not get killed crossing the busy street in front of the clinic.

The good ol' days of nursing are a stark contrast to today, and in most ways, it was better back then. Now, our clinic's priorities are heading in a very scary direction:

```
To: KatrinkaC@MeHosp.org
From: GloriaT@MeHosp.org
    BIG boss is here. Inspection. Look busy. Beeper
meeting later.
    Gloria
```

P.S.—Don't worry about patient. "Hang in there"
doesn't always inspire suicide. Just tidy up med closet.

9:33 a.m.

To: KatrinkaC@MeHosp.org
From: GloriaT@MeHosp.org

P.S.—Nellie's going to Great-Full Bakery. Want
something?

Absolutely NOT. Today starts my new diet.

9:34 a.m.

To: GloriaT@MeHosp.org
From: KatrinkaC@MeHosp.org

Cinnamon roll.

—T.

P.S.—Tell Nellie to try to find out if that nice
lady who works there is single. For my <u>brother</u>.

My longtime work friend Nellie makes frequent runs to the
bakery and is still super-skinny. And tall, dammit, but I like her anyway.
She used to be a model, so I made her promise me that when my time
comes to pass from this world, she will personally make sure they use all
my own makeup on me for the final "show." After all, I wouldn't want
someone else's colors on me. She understands that. I paid $40 for that
color thing back in the '80s. Let me go to eternity in peace as a "Winter."

Feeling a little guilty about the cinnamon roll I can't wait to eat,
I fire off an e-mail to Ben, who's upstairs in the same building.

9:35 a.m.

To: BenL@MeHosp.org

From: KatrinkaC@MeHosp.org

How's it going on your floor? Miss you. Hey—can you pick up some *decaf* tea bags, some fruit, maybe a bag of those fresh pea pods or green beans— something healthy when you shop later?

Get off fat ass and walk. No more cinn. rolls.
No choc. truffle unless walk 20" 1st. Only 1 pt
Haagen-Dazs *per mos. Every oth mos. Every 6*
wks. 5 to 6. Every 5 wks.

And can you also get a pint of Haagen-Dazs chocolate chocolate chip ice cream, just *for emergencies*. Like in case your family stops by. Chocolate chocolate chip. Haagen-Dazs. Only that kind. If they have it.

xoxox Tink

Oh.

P.S.—Can you pick up the groceries after work & drop them back home before you and your brother go out to your Men's Club later? I.O.U.!

—T.

The rest of the day flies by in a flurry of the usual incoming calls and paperwork, more than humanly possible to get through, even on a good day. That cinnamon roll was a good idea, as lunch consisted of an old, dry, half-eaten granola bar, an apple, and tea. Not exactly good nutrition, overall. But tonight's sub sandwich night, lots of veggies.

…how to gain peace-filled, happy existence and still enjoy food…

~ ~ ~ ~ ~ ~ ~ ~

8:25 p.m.

Quick stop, grocery store. Should have mentioned lite popcorn and mini-carrots to Ben—run in quick—oh, GOD, why do they put those very freshly baked, lightly glazed donuts by the front entrance?!? Just ignore—mouth breathe—keep moving. Four people ahead of me in Express Lane, woman in front of me reeking of garlic (good for her and her heart health, but it's making me nauseated) and booze-breath man behind me. The slowest teenage cashier possible—oh, how I want those donuts, all cotton-candy tasting, all I need is one—why sold in 10-packs all glorious and inviting?—stick with carrots and popcorn—will this line EVER move?

I turn to the man behind me to give him a well-deserved glare, but it's wasted on the loaded old coot. He smiles his glassy red-eyed grin at me (oh, great—he likes me). Can't he just hold his breath? I'm dying here.

Waiting. Waiting. Spice Woman needs cigarettes, which are locked up and now the cashier has to flick on her light to get the manager to help. Ugh…damn donuts. Well, maybe at home, just a spoonful of Haagen-Dazs, just a spoonful, enough to induce feeling of peace…

Usually I am not this crabby inside. Really. Only yesterday I stopped at this very store for a couple of quick things, and in back of me was a young mom with two babies, about a year apart. So adorable, and both fussing in tandem, and I insisted the woman go before me and I even helped keep the older one busy with a bunch of my goofiest faces. Good princess, for a moment. So there.

And finally? Home. Just pulling into the driveway feels so good…

…until I see the empty container of Haagen-Dazs taunting me from the top of the kitchen garbage.

9 p.m.

Ben—Sweetie—WHAT THE HELL HAPPENED
TO THE ICE CREAM?!?
Did you actually let your pig of a brother eat it
when he was here?!?
Love,
Tink
P.S.—Going to bed early. Heartbreak.

Before I go to bed, I scan the newest pile of mail.

BIG DEAL BOOK CLUB
MARGERY CASAWILL!
Join today and you'll receive an Overnight Bag...the perfect way to carry all your belongings...

Damn! I hate these stupid...Well, the thing is, my mother would have loved getting a free overnight bag. I remember our frequent trips to the department store makeup counters. She'd buy $100 worth of makeup just to get the free mini tote bag of samples, and I'd tease her about how much she'd spent to "look youthful at any age!" just because she thought I might want a new lipstick shade, and she or I wanted the tote.

Ring. Ring. Beep. "Hi. It's Tink. Leave a message."
"Tink—It's Lorraine. Hey—as long as you're sorting through the teacups, can you see if your mom's locket is around somewhere? Talk soon!" *Click.*

Ring. Ring. Beep. "Hi. It's Tink. Leave a message."

"Tink? Hey—it's Richard. Your brother. Think I'll come visit in a few days. How about getting me a date? Call me."

Click.

Well…I might be able to find someone nice, but probably not that quickly. Ugh. One more thing.

Exactly what happened to the idea of getting more rest and taking care of myself? Oh, yeah. *Other people.* Not feeling that special urge to be a hero at the moment. Not acting princess-like. More like Wicked Witch.

In the background, I hear Ben come home. Now I wish I hadn't left that note for him, although Ben misses a lot, so he probably didn't even see it.

Another call from Lorraine.

"Tink? Hey, your dad just called me. He can't find his nail clippers. Can you call him? Not much I can do from Pennsylvania."

Shit. He's not even supposed to *have* nail clippers.

I e-mail Fr. Rob, asking for prayers or a one-way bus ticket to his friary. Do they take women?

I pick up the phone to call the front desk at Gorgeous Ageless Gardens to get someone to look into the Great Nail Clipper Mystery. Then I go find Ben to snuggle, and find him sitting in the downstairs den, listening to The Band and strumming his Gibson. I sit next to him, rubbing the back of his neck. Sometimes rubbing him soothes me. He turns toward me and makes a lazy half-smile, and makes a little kiss toward my direction. And I wonder when my emotions, hormones, and outside pressures will calm down.

And how long it will be before I stop thinking about the missing ice cream and the glazed donuts.

{CHAPTER 7}

In which our hero struggles against forces of the workplace.

The next day: a case of contagious work crap.

> **To: All Outpatient Staff**
> **From: MyersE@MeHosp.org**
>
> First, thanks in advance to all staff members who have already participated in the staff satisfaction survey. To those who haven't, I look forward to your input.
>
> Second, your Employee Safety Test must be done by the end of the week. Use the Hospital Intranet. Click on "Annual Safety Test." It is mandatory and is part of your Annual Review.
>
> Finally, we are pleased to formally announce that all staff will carry beepers for patient safety and dissemination of information. We will notify you by floor when the beepers arrive, with printouts available listing all staff names, beeper numbers, and home phone numbers.

Great. Like we're not at management's beck and call enough? Well, maybe it won't be so bad. I mean, they can't really expect us to be on call 24/7.

My cell phone is going off—somewhere in my humongous pocketbook. I only use it for emergencies. The family and my dad's caregivers are aware of that. I freak out when I get calls on my cell, ever since my mom was so sick. It was always bad news, like the time she fell and we went along in the rescue truck to the hospital, where she ended up for ten days. It was awful. We were so worried she wouldn't pull through. Then later, there was the phone call that came in at 3 a.m. from the nursing home. It was the first time in my life I could not catch my breath for what seemed like an eternity. Mom had taken a turn for the worse, we "should come, it could be any time now." I woke up everyone, pulled them from sleep. We looked like hell and gathered at her bedside. She hung on for a few more days, until the end.

Ever since, I've been terrified whenever the cell phone goes off. And now the damn thing's ringing off the hook and I can't find—

"Hello?!?!" I am practically hyperventilating.

Too late. But someone's left a message.

I go through tapping in a bunch of numbers to retrieve the message, first all the wrong ones, then finally the right ones. I feel my heart rate rising. It's from my cousin. Oh, God, I hope she's OK. I tap in the numbers. Oh, Lorraine, please be OK, please be—

"Hi, Tink? It's Lorraine. Hey, I hear Richard is seeing you guys this weekend and you might be finding him a date. Can you ask Ben if he has a nice friend for me for the next time I come to visit?" *Click.*

Breathe in…breathe out…loving…giving…breathe…

The workday with its influx of calls and paperwork demands makes me wonder what nursing has turned into. Plus, I can't get my lousy computer to work right. My printer doesn't work at all, but I'm used to that. My brain hurts.

Then, for a moment, I smile, then giggle aloud as I remember stopping at Starbucks this morning. Mark, a young guy I've known a couple of years, always makes my special drink perfectly. This morning, he drew a heart on top of the whipped cream with chocolate drizzle.

Hey, maybe Little Tink and he…well, anyway. I look around, and still chuckling, notice Dr. Myers is standing in the doorway, eyeing me suspiciously. Oh, for God's sake. Around here, if you show a moment of joy, someone thinks you've gone batty. I turn to my computer. God! I can't stand it.

~ ~ ~ ~ ~ ~ ~ ~

To: All Outpatient Staff
From: MyersE@MeHosp.org

We are experiencing hospital-wide computer issues and are working very hard to resolve this. Although the regular e-mail system works, the Internet as well as the Hospital Intranet is down. We will…

Blah, blah, blah—

…major rebuilding efforts…

Blah, blah—

…in-house Computer Specialists…

God, please make him stop!

…early next week, at the latest…

Gonna hang myself…

…extending the deadline for completing your Employee Safety Test for a period of 24 hours after…

I shut the screen off.

I turn it back on.

It's still there.

…Unfortunately, the software itself is time-limited. I have attached a check-in rotation schedule including night shift and a phone notification list…

Z-z-z-z-z-z-z...

...Reminder: It is mandatory, and part of our hospital's Trot to Excellence campaign.

Please pick up your beeper according to the schedule in your mailbox. Thank you all for your cooper—

Delete.

Wonderful. Can't wait for a beeper interruption in the two minutes of free time I have with Ben.

> **To: MyersE@MeHosp.org**
>
> **From: KatrinkaC@MeHosp.org**
>
> Ernie, re safety test schedule—I won't be around this weekend—have to go to my parents' condo—big move coming up.
>
> Tink

AUTOMESSAGE:

Dr. Ernest Myers is currently out of the office.

OK, I know he's here. Eyeballing staff to make sure everything remains boring and joyless.

~ ~ ~ ~ ~ ~ ~ ~

So, the beepers arrive for "scheduled pick-up." Can't anything ever be casual or spontaneous here? It's a hospital, for God's sake— *human services*. Everyone is unhappy about the beepers, and now the administrators can call us anytime.

And I get reprimanded by my nursing supervisor, Gloria (what?!?—I am never having fun with her again) because Lorraine (!)

calls our clinic Operator and leaves this message in the general voicemail: "Well, this isn't exactly an emergency, unless you consider no dates and no sex for two months an emergency. But could you ask Tink Casawill to call me? It's her cousin Lorraine."

To: All Outpatient Staff
From: MyersE@MeHosp.org

Oh, no. Not again.

Reminder: Effective immediately, all staff must wear their beepers unless they are observing a religious holiday. Religious holiday observance must be approved by your supervisor at least two days prior to the holiday, so that special coverage can be obtained while you are off-beeper.
Thank you for your cooperation.

Dr. Myers. Just what cereal box did they pull him out of? Is there a human there? Isn't there a fairy tale about someone captured by an alien life form…brainwashed…spit out as a supervisor…Evidence: every single day, he eats the exact same lunch—an American cheese sandwich on white bread with mustard. Every. Day.

Enough said.

Later, in my mailbox, I find the annually distributed "Respect Policy." Big institutions, big initiatives, gotta cover that big corporate ass. I know we'll group-read, review, and get quizzed on it at a Friday morning meeting.

Respect? I'll tell you what respect is. Respect is not waking me up to review the damn Respect Policy while I'm trying to get some rest during a staff meeting.

Problem: I'm officially at an age where I call everyone "honey." I can't help it. It's that perimenopause crap again. In the midst of this ridiculously busy workday, one of the secretaries goes out of her way to help me, with the kindest, most soothing voice I've heard in a long while.

"Thank you, honey," I say, before I know what's coming through my mouth.

I know I'm not supposed to call anyone "honey" at work. It's just that my brain is filled with "grandma" hormone. It's the same stuff that makes me stop to admire every yummy, chubby-cheeked, drooling baby I see, and then get pissed off at bad drivers and, you know, lean on my horn for an obnoxiously long time. So now I have to watch what I say. Don't want to violate the fucking Respect Policy.

No admin. a—holes for Little T.

Good humans only!!!

6:30 p.m.

Home at last. I'm beat.

Ah. Another Sisters of Our Most Precious Lord mailing.

~REFLECTIONS FROM THE SISTERS OF
OUR MOST PRECIOUS LORD~
JOIN US FOR OUR SPECIAL
SPIRITUAL DAY!
DETAILS INSIDE:

There is a quiet time for our hearts to ponder
the wonders of our Lord...as we formulate our
mission and make our decisions as a reverent
group of...

Sorry, good Sisters, but I can't look at a thick mailing right now.

Probably nothing important. I'll just say a prayer for them before bed. That would feel very faith-filled. *And maybe get me on the road to peacefulness…gratitude…*

{CHAPTER 8}

A glimpse of our hero's struggle with hormones and mornings.

Maybe I was getting a little extra moody. *SO. WHAT.*

I love Ben, but does he have to be such a *morning* person every day?!?

I stay up late doing all the things I have to get done and then he's up bright and early and WHISTLING, for God's sake at, like, 6 a.m. and leaves early for work—

Oh, crap.

I forgot about the weekly Friday morning meeting.

I wonder if Fr. Rob got my e-mail about praying for me. Well, the weekend's coming. A chance to just hang out.

Katrinka finds herself in the dangerous land of crack.

Weekend!!!!!

I feel like dancing! I want to sing! Shop! Eat out! Go to the mall!

Yes! THE MALL!!!!!

God. Almighty.

Why, why, WHY must we be forced to look at the ass cracks of total strangers? It used to be enough that once in a while we needed to call a plumber. Talk about your ugly eyeful, just to get the sink fixed. But now *women* in all areas of life—libraries, schools, the mall…I mean, I am going along, minding my own business (OK, maybe I don't mind my own business, but still) and then there it is, right in my path, possibly up to four full inches of someone's crack. I especially hate it—it's just downright nauseating—if it's my waitress. *I'm trying to eat.*

The rest of the mall experience goes downhill from there.

I mean, do they ever clean the public restrooms? It's bad enough that restrooms sometimes smell really bad. I get that. But do people not know how to flush? And hand-washing has just gone down the drain, no pun intended. That's what's wrong with people. Wash! Flush and wash.

I walk through the aisle of kiosks at the mall and am accosted by salespeople. One steps toward me as I pass by. "Excuse me, can I ask you a question?" he asks, with an exotic accent. I fall for it. He pulls me toward him by the arm and starts to hold a hot/cold herbal pack to my neck, asking "Do you have any aches or pains?"

"Just you," I mutter, as I escape with my wallet intact. Only to be jumped, moments later, by another voice, an outstretched arm, holding a cell phone: "I can give you a better monthly deal!"

Where are salespeople when you really need one, like when you're wandering around a huge store looking for a particular item and there is NO ONE available and you have a headache plus you're hungry because the lunch you were going to take to work got left sitting on the kitchen counter to spoil or when the only salesperson on the floor is having an intense conversation with someone on a cell phone by her cash register involving what side dish to bring to the family picnic?!?

(Definitely, potato salad.)

...*deep breath*...

My trip to the mall makes me want to go home and shower.

~ ~ ~ ~ ~ ~ ~ ~

...and now, back to a place of peacefulness, cleverly masked as chaos...

I get home to find that Ben has actually cleared off the kitchen table. Nice. Maybe we'll play checkers later, now that there's some space. But he's nowhere to be found. Oh, and I guess he finally found my note from the other day.

*Tink—I thought the ice cream was for company!
I'll get more. But that reminds me. I've been
meaning to ask you—will you marry me?
—Ben
P.S.—Come to bed.*

Um—*really?* My heart is melting and pounding at the same time. He's the sweetest guy in the world. One thing about being late-in-life partners is that we can really talk and support each other. And true, we're engaged, but I thought that would be enough, at least for the time being. Like 20 years.

I want to know someone well enough and long enough to see what's there after the initial giddiness wears off, to see what else there is to him. And to see what's left of myself.

I go upstairs and give him a hug and a kiss.

"I saw your note," I say. "What's the deadline for a yes or no? I mean, do I have enough time to take a Valium?" He chuckles and kisses the top of my head (I love that), then picks up the novel he's reading and sits in the comfy chair in our bedroom.

I briefly check for any urgent phone messages, in case my dad has called.

"Aunt T? It's Little T! I got a call-back for a small part in an off-Broadway show! I owe it all to you!! Mmmmwahhh!" *Click.*

and:

"Mom? It's Ali. Lorraine said you're sorting through Gaga's stuff. That must be hard for you, Mom. Lorraine said everyone should let you know what they want. What I really want—is Gaga…"

Oh, God. My chest literally starts aching.

"…but…well…watch for the pink-flowered teacup for me. It

will remind me of her when I use it. Oh—and Elliott and Katie would enjoy some of the old VHS movies. Hey, wait a sec. Katie? Spell video, please. V-I-D…good. Keep going. Sorry, hold on, Mom— E— right! What's next?"

I'm pretty sure it's "O," I'm thinking.

"…Katie? Katie? Come on, honey. You're doing grea— *BEEEEEEEP!" Click.*

then:

"Hi. It's Little T. About that show. It *closed*! (sniff) I'm so upset! Can you call me?" *Click.*

Oh…Little Tink. I've watched her career since she was a little kid in summer stock and I've seen the hard work she's done. I'll have to remember to call her later. Yeah, I'll call her back, and we'll chat like we've done so many times before. I don't know if it's ever helped her much, but at least she knows I love her and care about her.

Then I send out a quick e-mail to the family:

> Hi, everyone.
>
> I'm a little overwhelmed right now with work, financial and legal things for Gaga's estate and such. So I won't be able to sort through belongings right away—sorry. But anyone who wants to come up to help or look through stuff is welcome to do so.
> Love,
> Aunt Tink/Mom/Grandma, etc.

And then, well, it's as I send the e-mail off to everyone and prepare to pay bills related to Mom's death and my dad's living expenses that I remember, like some kind of big Freudian space-out, that TOMORROW is moving day at the condo. Holy. God.

I no sooner send the family e-mail off and my Inbox is, like, on fire.

> **To: Tink@maine.com**
> **From: RichardC@NHschool.org**
>
> Cool! Save me some of Mom's old makeup and stationery for my daughters, OK?
>
> Richard

> **To: Tink@maine.com**
> **From: John@NC.com**
>
> Tink, I think it would really mean a lot to Ali if, when you do go through everything, you could set aside a few pieces of "Gaga" memories for her. She misses her so much. And maybe some nice photographs. Later. I know you're busy. Maybe you could just keep a little list somewhere of these kinds of requests, you know? Studies show that making lists keeps people organized during stressful times.
>
> Love,
>
> Your favorite son-in-law, John

Crap.

Wait.

Favorite?

It does not escape my tired brain that part of my effort to take on too much is connected with the princess yearnings, and underlying that, the need to be liked. How to reconcile that is another story.

> **To: John@NC.com**
> **From: Tink@maine.com**

John, great! I'll see what I can do.

Your favorite mother-in-law,

Tink

I head toward the bedroom and the phone rings. I keep walking.

Princesses must learn to ignore some of the minor distractions of life in order to deal with loftier things.

Ring. Ring. Beep. "Hi. It's Tink. Leave a message."

"Hi, Aunt T! It's Little T. You don't need to call me back. I just got an e-mail from my agent about some upcoming auditions, so I'm good. But did I hear you're taking requests for what each of us wants from Gaga's? I'll take ANYTHING connected to music and theater. Even clothing for costumes. Love you!" *Click.*

Ring. Ring. Beep. "Hi. It's Tink. Leave a message."

"Mom? It's Dylan. Uh, I don't think I can fit much from the condo into my dorm room. But maybe I can help you sort some stuff next time I come up. Would that help? Yeah, anyway, I gotta go—have a paper due tomorrow. Tell Ben I said hi. Love you, Mom."

So sweet. And you know what? I'm going to just take care of myself right now. Take a little personal time. I don't have to—

Ring. Ring. Beep. "Hi. It's Tink. Leave a message."

"Tink? Ben? Did I get the right num— oh, shoot. Well, it's Dad. Your dad—over at the…the…well, someone here said something about Bingo. Or, wait. Was it Bingo or…oh, damn. CAN YOU CALL ME? I'm…I'm all mixed up. It's Dad." Click.

I check the clock. 11:30 p.m. I look into the bedroom. Ben's snoring.

It's worth the short drive. True, I have to stop for gas. And true, it's so late I have to practically go across town to find a pump open, and true, by the time I get to Gorgeous Ageless Gardens, he's almost asleep. I let myself into his room, and am hit with a familiar subtle mixture of bathroom cleanser and nice Dad scent of suits and coats from long ago. He perks up and grins at me from his lounger.

"Tink—you're here!"

Anyway, turns out he played Bingo for the first time in his life and made $32, and he just can't make sense of it. It doesn't help any that he played, or tried to play, four cards at once. And he wants to give me the money.

"You keep it, Dad. It's like allowance. Remember Mom used to give you thirteen dollars a week allowance and you never spent it?"

And true, it makes him—and me—cry. The Bingo, the winnings, the memories of Mom giving him an allowance…but I can't very well ignore him when he's all mixed up, can I?

When I leave, I advise him to only play one card at a time. And I hug him. And hug him again. In spite of his aging, thinning body, he still has a surprisingly strong hug. I tell him I love him.

He smiles up at me with those beautiful, shining blue eyes. "OK," he says, looking more settled, "just one card. One Bingo card. OK!"

~ ~ ~ ~ ~ ~ ~ ~

The next morning, at the condo, Ben and I meet up with the movers, five men and one woman, all T-shirted in blue-and-white company-name uniforms that advertise their promise to "get the job done right." Sounds good to me.

Somehow, six rooms of furnishings, plus exactly 73 drawers and boxes and bins of house wares, clothes, linens, paper, junk, and more, some looking remarkably important, get transported to the waiting storage units. At first, the movers take the boxes I've previously packed and labeled. I thought I'd done so much over the last several weeks, with Ben and Richard's help. But it turns out we only did a fraction of the job, so now the movers are just packing stuff up like a SWAT team "getting the job—blah, blah, blah," and any sense of order or labeling has come to an end. Richard shows up later in the day, after he gets out of work, and my friend Adeline, a psychic reader, comes over.

I get the slow realization that what I thought would be oh-so-carefully organized is now a complete train wreck, packed nice and tight, literally to the ceiling, into two 10′x 15′ storage units.

"I sensed you needed some help, sweetie," she says, and hands me a small but really good quality French chocolate bar.

I'm going to need a whole lot more than chocolate. But it's a start. I hug her for her thoughtfulness, and for a moment, I feel my breath catch as I take in the reason for all this moving. I use everything I have to keep breathing, to take a few slow breaths. Because if I don't, I'm going to cry. And if I start crying, I may never stop.

{CHAPTER 10}

Our hero is kept on indefinite hold with an insurance company, listening to a Muzak version of The Beatles' "Why Don't We Do It in the Road?" complete with a string orchestra and a 100-voice chorus.

Phone to ear most of the day, I might get two minutes, total, to talk to my lovely patients. It's all about insurance now.

I'm on hold again. I could *make* the pills people need in the time I'm waiting to process an insurance approval.

"...Please hold for the next available case management associate...(music) 'no one will be watching us...' Please continue to hold while our associates are assisting other health professionals...(music) 'Why don't we do it in...'"

I'm thinking, Why don't YOU friggin' do it to yourselves in the road? when the line is answered by a teenager with no medical background.

I am getting seriously cranky. And I do not think it's hormonal. So *shut*...never mind.

I feel like a pusher. Might as well be standing on a darkened street corner. "Yeah, she really needs it. Like, can you give her a few pills now and de rest later? Uh, yeah, sure she tried dat one, but uh, no, it didn't work. Nope. Look, just give us ten of them, just ten for thirty days, we'll stretch it. Ten, dammit, ten. You owe me that much. And nobody gets hurt."

The doctor and patient no longer decide. The insurance industry and the government do. Depending on what deals they make.

Ugh. These people.

I have to rest my hormones now.

But first, I'll just check my—

To: KatrinkaC@MeHosp.org
From: MyersE@MeHosp.org

    Tink, I'm afraid "keeping the Lord in my heart every day" does not qualify as a "continuous holiday observance," nor does it exempt you from carrying a beeper.

Oh, come on. Isn't there something called time off in our country?!?

~ ~ ~ ~ ~ ~ ~ ~

It's been a very long day.

At 7:15 p.m., I am in the middle of the grief group I've joined. (Oh, how I miss my mother. I would have been at a movie with her, popcorn box in hand and giggling as I surreptitiously passed her dark chocolate truffles, not sitting with a nice group of very sad people with Kleenex boxes around the circle and a candle burning in the middle.) That's when my beeper goes off, mere hours after I finally sign it out. Ten years ago, I'd have thought it was cool to carry a beeper. That was when I had free time. Now I need an extra hour a day in the bathroom because—oh, never mind. I leave the group to return the call.

Turns out a clinic patient I don't even know is in the ER, and the staff is trying to get a med list to evaluate for a side effect: dry mouth. Would I go to the clinic and look it up on the computer? What? Are they kidding? I believe the words "when pigs fly out your ass, jerk-off!" are uttered by someone who has temporarily inhabited my body. Then—too late—it occurs to me that maybe that wasn't a cool response and I might get reported to my boss at the clinic. Well, if it gets back to him, I'll just make something up that doesn't sound too bad, like temporary insanity.

Dr. Myers beeps me 32 minutes later, as the group leader is reading the closing meditation.

Apparently he didn't realize that a woman who communes daily with the Lord could come up with all those words that do not fit in with our hospital's Respect Policy.

He could have at least offered me a day off to de-stress.

I told you. It really is that perimenopause thing. I'm sure of it. 'Cause I'm a half inch away from my period at this moment. I'm bitchy, I'm emotional, I'm starving, and yeah, my breasts are sore. Because I will NOT give up all my caffeine, dammit!

OK, maybe I will. For a few days. But not now, not when I'm this hormonal.

8:30 p.m. Home, checking mail.

I take this cheery yellow postcard and throw it. It flies through the air, taunting me, and lands not even close to the trash.

Upstairs, I send off a quick e-mail to Fr. Rob, then take a long bath. Ben pokes his head in and asks me if I want him to wash my back. And the rest, I won't divulge. But during the ensuing hour, he brings up the marriage idea, which, I must admit, is very appealing. I mean, his timing is exquisite.

~ ~ ~ ~ ~ ~ ~ ~

Midnight. One last check of my e-mails.

I see Fr. Rob has already responded to an earlier, um, spontaneous e-mail I sent him.

> **To: Tink@maine.com**
> **From: FrRob@StPeter.org**
>
> Nice to hear from you again. ☺
>
> All is well here. Always happy to give you spiritual guidance. ☺
>
> To answer your question, I think it is probably OK to use foul language at times ☺ as long as it is not the Lord's name in vain ☹ ! But yes, I agree that I would try not to use it in front of children or your patients. ☺
>
> Are you OK? Sound a little overwhelmed.
>
> My best to your family,
>
> Fr. Rob

I barely make it to bed without my eyes clicking shut like one of those old baby dolls from childhood. Business matters can wait. Everything will be fine.

Rest…peace…renewal…good princ—…z-z-z-z-z-z.

{CHAPTER 11}

We pause, once again, whilst our hero contemplates the meaning of womanhood.

Hormones, young and old.

I *SAID* I have PMS and I'm Not Kidding.

OK, don't skip this part. Get a little snack to eat while you're reading. Maybe a nice piece of fruit. Wash it first.

In fifth grade, we girls were ushered into the school auditorium and shown THE FILM that held the secret to our exciting female future. As a few curious boys strained at the rear windows of the darkened auditorium, we sat and watched our instructional presentation, which was a plumbing film that told us nothing about being female.

The lights went up.

"Any questions?" yawned the scrawny, graying school nurse, whom we suspected only pretended to be a female itself. She was the most sexless creature created on two legs. No way could we ask a question of the woman who responded to any ailment we had with her own question: "Have you moved your bowels this morning?"

She'd hand us a magazine and point to the tiny bathroom behind her desk in her nurse's office. (OK. Sometimes it helped. But still.)

So there we girls were, in the auditorium, being handed a pamphlet called "Growing Up and Liking It." It was an effort by a sanitary napkin company to hook our business. Most of us were too excited and curious about the thought of actively growing breasts and wearing a bra (so grown up!) to question whether the other aspects of femaleness might not be all that much fun. In fact, we might not "Like

It" at all. Fortunately, my mother was very open and natural about all that stuff, so becoming a woman was exciting and not traumatic. Then again, her perception of some things was a little skewed. Like in regard to childbirth, she told me labor was like "menstrual cramps." Oh, hahahahahahaha!!!! My ex-husband also thought her version of childbirth was a bit off after I dug my nails into him during "transition," just before Ali was born. Just like menstrual cramps? There's a man walking around today with scars to disprove that one.

But what my mom totally left out was this perimenopausal junk. I don't recall her mentioning it. Oh, wait. She did. I remember now. She said, "Eh, I had a couple of hot flashes. Felt nice and warm for a minute. That was all." OK. I'm not trying to imply that my wonderful mother was a liar. No, she was very ethical. But she must have had one heck of an accommodating body. Or some incredible drugs. Now that I think about it, she was awfully pleasant. Oh, and there's something else she left out. But I can't talk about it.

Note to any males who might be reading this: Women realize life is just as difficult for men as for women. Now please close this book and go do something else. Like hammer some wood together. I'm trying to talk to my girlfriends. Thank you.

I'm not bashing men. Not at all. I *like* them. Except for once in a while, when they can't read my mind.

I know. I can't understand it either.

{CHAPTER 12}

Katrinka becomes immersed in her calling.

Like any other busy morning, I check e-mails between dressing and getting a quick breakfast for the road.

New plan—take care/self—truly capable non-hyster, non-dessert-crav. ?change/life?

To: Tink@maine.com

From: LittleTink@NY.com

hi, aunt T! i gave your e-mail address to my friend Annie—hope you don't mind, she's going through a hard time with this guy gary—a real prick of a boyfriend.

Love,

LT

Three minutes later, as I realize I need to hurry up or be late for work again, I get an e-mail from "Annie," who sounds like a nice young woman asking only for her boyfriend to be a little more sensitive. Apparently, he gave her a tool kit for her birthday. Not even the good brand with a lifetime guarantee. Cheapo.

To hell with punching the time clock. This is more important. I tell her to go out and do something nice for herself, forgive him when she's ready, and remember she has to love herself before she can love someone else. I know. It's bullshit. But I read it somewhere and it sounds smart. Then I tell her to make sure she reads a good book on home repairs before she ever tries to fix something. And I warn her not to do anything with electricity. You need a professional for that shit.

Hurrying now—makeup, earrings, quick check in mirror—hate that midriff bulge thing—just makes me feel more guilty about eating—which probably increases belly fat hormone—God, I hate a little bit of knowledge and why can't it be like it was 20 years ago—I could eat anything it didn't matter—I was healthy, thin, pretty, relaxed…I keep going, pass by the ringing phone as I head downstairs—briefly pause to listen…

Ring. Ring. Beep. "Hi. It's Tink. Leave a message."

"Tink? It's Richard. Hey, I was just thinking about all the hard work you do every day as a nurse…"

God, he's a sweetie…

"Remember when you were so worried about me when I was a kid and I hurt my leg at the state park? You were so sweet…"

Oh, wow…

"I think you were only about five—just like a little nurse. So—uh—I was wondering—do you have any cute nurse friends for me to meet?" *Click.*

I keep going. Toast. Wheat toast. Whole wheat. Heading out for another action-packed day as SuperNurse. You've seen her before—the efficient, good-humored one with the heart of gold and the annually expanding waistline.

~ ~ ~ ~ ~ ~ ~ ~

Many people ask me why I became a nurse.

OK, maybe only four or five. But anyway.

In spite of having a very sweet but completely ignorant school nurse as my earliest role model (I mean, come on. Did she really think my menstrual cramps began the exact moment final exams started in my high school freshman year?!?), I became a nurse. Truthfully, there was another nurse I remember, many years ago, from my pediatrician's office. Nice, very pretty, wore white, including the traditional starched white cap. Now *that* was a *nurse*. In college, I studied childhood education freshman year. But then I got a summer job at a local nursing home. The littlest things made the patients so happy. I remember Anna Marie, a sweet old woman, her overweight husband long gone from cardiac disease, her children and grandchildren halfway across the country. Anna Marie had several medical problems and needed a lot of assistance with moving around, but was otherwise in good shape. Mentally, I think she was sharper than I was back in those hectic young-adult days of working in the daytime and partying at night.

Her visitors were few, but she would light up at the tiniest things—a letter, a phone call…One day I had some extra time, so I sat with her and we had tea and shortbread cookies together that her daughter had sent her. She told me about growing up in the era before TV, living on a big farm in upstate New York, and she showed me a small photo album she had that included pictures of her as a young girl. Dentures clicking quietly, she talked of simpler times, then asked for a second cup of tea, and eventually needed to take a nap. I visited her on the next vacation home from school. She lit right up, and we had tea again, this time me filling her in on my experiences away at college. In my sophomore year, I became a nursing major and never looked back. I truly enjoyed the privilege of caring for others. And I looked great in white.

But things are so different now. Most of my nursing career was extremely fulfilling. It is no small thing to ease someone's pain, provide those things we call comfort. But now? Hospitals are, like, all business. We're always understaffed. So even when I'm worn down by all the paperwork and administrative demands, I still have to drum up a lot of caring and compassion.

It just never fucking stops.

Just one lone e-mail greets me at night:

> **To: Tink@maine.com**
> **From: RealGuy@man.com**
>
> Aunt Tink—who do you think you are telling Annie to put her needs first—what kind of a person are you anyway—did she pay you for this BS?! We were fine 'til you had to butt in—
>
> —Gary

Oh, great.

reminder—treat self well dammit—set limits—find way to carefree life—why in NURSING???

{CHAPTER 13}

Sacrifices are rewarded.

Tink, hi! How's it going? Better, I hope! ☺ ☺
Keeping you in my prayers! Thinking of visiting
Maine on my next time off.

~Fr. Rob

Ring. Ring. Beep. "Hi. It's Tink. Leave a message."

"Grandma? It's Katie. Guess what? I got a hundred on my spelling test. A *hundred*! That's H-U-N-D-R-E-D." *Click.*

Ring. Ring. Beep. "Hi. It's Tink. Leave a message."

"Hi, Mom! It's Dylan. What's up? Hey—I was just wondering—can you look and see if my tux is hanging up somewhere? I'm emceeing a fundraiser here at school next weekend and it would be awesome to wear it. If it's not too much trouble. Just let me know. So, uh, thanks, Mom. Love you!" *Click.*

Oh! Of *course* I'll send it. Let's see…clean and press first. Drop off at cleaners before work. Already picturing him in it. My handsome boy…I'll never forget the first time he needed a tux, for his junior prom. We ended up buying one on sale instead of renting one. He just loved being dressed up, and had an adorable date for the prom. In his senior year, he used the tux a lot. He and his friends thought it was cool to get dressed up and go out, even if it was just for a pizza. His ironic "statement."

{Chapter 13}

Then it came time to get him ready for college. Preparation took weeks—shopping, sorting through things, whether to keep or bring or store. Endless piles of school papers, old socks from under his bed, teenage souvenirs, photos, posters…At first, I hid my growing sadness at his impending departure. He was, after all, my "baby"—all six feet of him. Then I achingly gave in and cried and hugged him, like, twice a week. Or maybe it was twice an hour; I can't remember. Poor kid put up with it and told me he'd miss me, too. Did he want to bring his tux to college? I asked him. No, he'd let me know if he needed it. So it hung in the laundry room where I could see it and wait for the next school vacation for his visit home. Now it gave me a chuckle to picture him in it at college, not just at the fundraiser. I figured he'd probably show up in class or the cafeteria wearing it.

I feel the tug of missing him mixed with pride.

It's been a good day.

{CHAPTER 14}

**Life takes some difficult turns. Katrinka recalls past traumas.
Much angst and shouting occur. The reader is advised to buckle up.**

Dumbo Insurance person: Thank you for calling CareLittle Rx. My name is Doris. Can I help you?

Me: Hi, Doris. I'm calling from—

Dumbo Doris: May I have your name and insurance policy number, please?

Me: Well, Doris, I'm calling from Dr. —

Dumbo: Policy number please?

Me: I don't have one. It. I mean, I'm a nurse—at a medical clinic. I'm calling on behalf of our patient Mrs. Fer—

Dumbo: Without the policy number, I cannot help you, ma'am.

Ten minutes later, "Doris" transfers me to another department so I can obtain the policy number of our sweet elderly patient who doesn't even know what company she now has, much less a policy number. But that was three phone calls ago.

I spend ten more minutes explaining a request for a medication not on their formulary.

Ten more minutes on hold, conversations with "Amber" and "Michelle," who explain, again, that the medication is not on their formulary, and the last one transfers me to someone who suggests trying a different medicine—a drug that is not even in the same category, with potentially deadly side effects.

Me: How did you get this job, you dickhead?

I'm kidding. I didn't say that.

Me: How did you get to be *in this position*, you dickhead? Do you have any medical background at all?

Kidding again. Ho-ho. What a joker.

Me: Can you please fax me the right form to fill out for this patient? It's urgent. If she can't get it refilled, SHE MAY END UP IN THE HOSPITAL.

The Latest Dumbo: Certainly. Let me put you on hold for —

That's when the line goes dead.

I start over.

Finally get the requisition form faxed to me, filled out, faxed back.

It's now in the hands of the insurance company's pharmacy "specialists" until a decision is made. Within 72 to 96 hours.

Meanwhile, they won't even be able to tell me when or if they receive my faxed form, because "it could be in any of our satellite offices." There are 64 of them.

> **To: KatrinkaC@MeHosp.org**
> **From: GloriaT@MeHosp.org**
> Sure, I'll contact the Department Chair for you about giving an in-service lecture. But change title—can't get Continuing Ed. credits for "Your Insurance Company is a Selfish A—hole."
> Gloria

Ohhhh…Ben just came in from his office and put a piece of dark chocolate in front of me. I can smell it through the wrapper. Like a heroin addict slamming in a fix, the bittersweet cocoa scent instantly makes me feel calmer. Ben looks around fast to make sure we're alone and gives me a little kiss. Would this stuff change if we got married?

Later, on the way home, I stop at the cleaner's to get Dylan's tux, anxious to tell my mom about—oh, God. Not again. A new wave of realization washes over me. I'm so used to talking with her, sharing family news. Now I can hear Mom's gentle reassurance: "I'm here. I'm still here," and can almost touch her presence.

Forcing my brain back to task, I make it just in time to the post office, put the tux into a box the size of Ohio so it doesn't get crushed, and mail it with Mommy Scrawl on the back of a paper bag I grabbed from the car's glove compartment, complete with the traditional "xoxox."

As I get back to my car, I see a little piece of paper tucked under my wiper. Huh? It's from Ben. Guess I missed seeing it when I left work. I love his little love notes.

Tink—I'll be late getting home—errands.
Love—Ben

Oh. I was going to cook dinner for us. Well…maybe we'll just have leftovers on our own.

~ ~ ~ ~ ~ ~ ~ ~

Friday night. Good to be home.

Ring. Ring. Beep. "Hi. It's Tink. Leave a message."

"Hi, Mom! It's Dylan. What's up? Uh, anyway, things are fine. I'm really, really busy, studying, like, *a lot*! But I wanted to tell you

I don't need the tux, so don't bother looking for it. We decided to do everything retro, so I'm actually using something from the theater department…Wait—hold up, guys. Sorry, Mom. Yeah, about the tux—thanks anyway. Talk to you soon. Love you!" *Click.*

Uh-huh.

The phone rings an hour and a half later. It's Ben. He's on his way home and do I want him to pick up something for me to eat? He already had something.

I make myself a big salad and toast and indulge in two back-to-back *Golden Girls* reruns, taking time to relax and pamper myself.

Later, I wrap myself in a cozy robe and gently submerge my tired feet into my little portable whirlpool tub in the bathroom. Comfy chair, feet warming in the bubbling water, nail polish and file on the side table next to me, just in case I feel like indulging. I lazily hold my pen and notebook on my lap. My beeper is on the floor nearby, but I'm really, really trying to not look down at it. I love my pretty bathroom, with the tiny pink-and-white bars of soap at the back of the tub—so different from the thick, square "Real Clean" moisturizing soap for men sitting on the counter.

> √ out nice pharmacist for Little T—
> single? √ left fing.

I look around the room while soaking. My eyes fix on the "manly" soap I picked up for Ben. Damn soap. Reminds me of Charlene and the shampoo.

You: Charlene? Who's Charlene? I don't recall seeing her on the character list.

Me: Don't start with me.

Charlene is my hairdresser. She works in a lovely, friendly little salon that, by the way, has a delightful restroom, AND she offers her customers a beverage upon entering the shop, and I can tell you that nice Charlene washes her pretty and talented little hands. And lotions them. No slouching there.

Now, I'm not saying I have a problem with spending $39.95 on a bottle of shampoo. After all, that was the "moderate" choice. There were some twice the price. Maybe it was from inhaling the nasal cacophony of hairspray, gels, and individual perfumes—but I made the mistake of asking, "Is there anything I can do for my hair? It's so dry lately."

From a distance, I hear the phone ring. Too bad. I'm relaxing. OK, and listening.

Ring. Ring. Beep. "Hi. It's Tink. Leave a message."

"Tink? It's Lorraine. I'm having second thoughts on which of your mom's teacups I want. Can you call me?" *Click.*

Accid. smash entire teacup coll. to smithereens—

Truly, I don't mind all these family calls. After all, they all just want a tangible reminder of our Gaga. I understand completely. No problem. It's actually wonderful and deeply moving.

OK, I got my period last night. So all is well…I love Ben, I love the world, I…well, that also reminds me of the thing I can't talk about.

{*Chapter 14*}

Oh, sorry.

Charlene.

Charlene's great. A sincere woman around 60 with the tidy little body of a 25-year-old—a woman full of wisdom...and, BTW, she never fails to ask me how Dylan's doing at school—she loves him almost as much as I do, and just from cutting his hair a few times. I would trust her to sell me an Edsel. And I'm not implying she would ever take advantage of me. On the contrary. She is caring and loving. But let's face it: hairdressers have this belief system about, well, hair. If your hair is very dry, they want to moisturize it. If it's oily, reduce the oil. Curly? Straighten it. Red? Lighten it. Brown? Redden it. Long? Cut it. It's like they can't stand to keep their hands off your hair.

Years ago, when I was chronically broke and single and raising a family, I noticed that a very exclusive hairdresser in town, a fellow from Austria, had a sign in the front window that read "Models Wanted." I discovered they held in-service classes to teach their employees the latest hairstyles. Basically, it was free if you let the proprietor cut and style your hair in front of the other hairdressers. This genius of a man took my out-of-control, long curly hair and cut it and styled it so beautifully that I felt—and looked—like a true princess. Six weeks later, when I wanted a trim, I called him up and volunteered to "model" again. This time, when I appeared with my shoulder-length hair, he said, almost aloud to himself, "I sink...shall ve brink it up to here?" and gestured knowingly with the sides of his hands to a place somewhere between my earlobe and the crown of my head.

In the distance, I hear my beeper going off. Should have left it at work.

Fuck it. I'm TAKING CARE OF MYSELF.

Oh, yeah. Free haircut.

That was the moment in which I could have run screaming from the shop.

Instead, intimidated by this "expert," I timidly asked, "Do you think it will look OK? I mean, my hair is awful curly. Frizzy, in fact."

"You'll luf it!" he beamed, practically dancing.

I'm not sure how to describe the feeling I had upon leaving his salon, but I'd say it was somewhere between complete panic and the sense one gets while searching for a method of suicide. Here I was with curly little locks on a thirty-something, slightly overweight face, my mother later exclaiming, "I *love* it! You look just like you did when you were a little girl!" and my children frankly laughing at me—just the vote of confidence I needed.

Rationalization being what it is, I told myself I'd adjust, that hair grows, that I could really work that head of hair daily and get it really cute…bought every product I could find, totaling roughly three times what a cut would have cost on the not-free market, in a effort to correct what I knew to be a nightmare look on me. My adult children, to this day, still can't resist, when a football game comes on TV, looking at me, then studying my face and hair pointedly, and asking, "Remember ven you hat zat football helmet look?"

Beeper is going off again.

Anyway. Charlene. So I said to her that my hair seemed dry and she pulled out no less than a dozen different shampoo brands ranging in price from very expensive to home-equity-loan range. I settled on the $39.95 bottle, which was, well, not very big but awfully pretty and purple and slender and all.

And I tried very hard not to think about the cost as I was charging it on my credit card that pays me back a whopping 3%. Or so they say.

You may think that I now obsessed about what I spent on the shampoo and couldn't enjoy luxuriating in it. Actually, no. My obsession ran in a different direction.

Me: Ben? (*I held up the pretty and purple and slender-and-all bottle.*) This is my new shampoo.

He: Good! I was going to tell you we're out of shampoo so you could pick some up at the big-box store when you get the dog food.

He won't shop at that big-box store, in protest against large conglomerates that put small places out of business. But don't even try to pass a big-box *hardware* store without stopping. The hypocrite.

The beeper again. Damn.

I grab it from the nearby table. It's the hospital. Ext. 51004.

Me: Hello? What is it?

Dr. Myers: Oh, hi, Tink. Nothing much. Just running a test of beepers. Random. Just testing.

Me: *It's eleven p.m.*

Dr. Myers: Right. Thanks for reminding me. I'm really beat. I'll just test out a few more and hang it up for the night.

So. Ben had pointed to the purple bottle of shampoo I was still holding in front of him.

He: That'll do, I guess. Don't much like the shape of the bottle, though.

I took a deep breath.

Me: No, uh, you see, Ben, this is *my* shampoo.

He: Well, it'll work OK for me, I suppose.

He walked off.

I went to the store that afternoon and picked up a big hulking bottle of shampoo on sale that actually carried the name of his favorite brand of soap on it. It was called "Real Clean and Manly Moisturizing Shampoo" or something like that. I think it had a picture of a penis on it.

Me: Here! (*I pulled it out of the bag.*) Shampoo!

He: Uh-huh…

He barely looked up.

Once I was sure, after additional instruction, that he knew which shampoo not to use, I stopped worrying so much.

Three days post purple-shampoo purchase, Ben was coming out of the shower.

He: I don't know about that purple shampoo there. It's not very good.

Um, Me: WHAT!?!?!? You're using my shampoo!?!?!? Do you have ANY IDEA HOW MUCH I PAID FOR THAT *PUNY* BOTTLE OF MIRACLE SOFTENING SHINY SHEEN SHAMPOO THAT IS *MINE* FOR *MY* HAIR?!?!?!?!?

He looked up at me.

He: Oh, it's just for you? I didn't know. I thought that other stuff you got from Big Ol' Mart might be too *whatever* for my hair. It says "moisturizing" on the label. I was just—

Me: THEY ALL SAY MOISTURIZING ON THE LABEL! THEY ARE TRYING TO SELL SHAMPOO! YOU USED MY $40 SHAMPOO ON YOUR SPARSE GRAY HAIR!!!!! *MY* SHAMPOO!!!!!!!!!!!!!!!!!!!!!!!!!!!!!!

He: Oh. Well, how does my hair look?

Well, better than mine did.

He: And the dog's coat?

I'm going back to the cheap stuff.

Take care of inner self—forget outwd. appear.

{ CHAPTER 15 }

OK.

Here it is. Just between us.
I found a gray hair.
Down there.

Ugh. My life is over.

{CHAPTER 16}

Reflections on spiritual connectedness.

~REFLECTIONS FROM THE SISTERS OF OUR MOST PRECIOUS LORD~

DEAR SISTERS AND ASSOCIATES, WARM AND LOVING GREETINGS, AND MAY THE SPIRIT OF OUR LORD SURROUND YOU! PLEASE TAKE THE TIME TO PRAYERFULLY LOOK OVER SOME OF THE WONDERFUL, INNOVATIVE OPTIONS WE WILL BE EXAMINING IN THE COMING MONTHS. ALTHOUGH LENGTHY, WE TRUST THAT THE LORD WILL GUIDE YOU INTO MANY MEDITATIVE MOMENTS OF DISCERNMENT AS YOU TAKE THIS PAGE BY PAGE, PARAGRAPH BY PARAGRAPH, SENTENCE BY SENTENCE, WORD BY —

Ring. Ring. Beep. "It's Tink. Leave a message."

"Tink? Richard. I know it's kinda late to be calling. Just came back from Prayer Group at my church…"

(See? You just can't find a guy as deep and thoughtful.)

"…and I was reminiscing about when you went to that Catholic college years ago. Remember that adorable, kind of sexy young nun there? Wow!" *Click.*

I'm sure I heard this wrong. I mean, Richard is totally wonderful.

To: Tink@maine.com
From: RealGuy@man.com

my girlfriend LEFT me—thanks a lot—now what? so upset I can barely eat.

—Gary

To: RealGuy@man.com
From: Tink@maine.com

Oh. Sorry. But wait. I'll bet your girlfriend—Annie, is it?—will come back to you. Then you can show her, once again, your true loving self.

(Hmm…that is, if you can even see her from the vantage point of having your head stuck up your ass.)

Meanwhile, Gary, have some chicken soup. And a few crackers. Very soothing.

"Aunt" Tink

To: FrRob@StPeter.org
From: Tink@maine.com

Hi, Fr. Rob. I'm just not having that loving and kind thing going on. And I wonder why God made me such a bitch.

In peace,

Tink

To: FrRob@StPeter.org
From: Tink@maine.com

P.S.—Oops. Really sorry—the b-word and all.

Tink ☺

To: Tink@maine.com
From: FrRob@StPeter.org

Don't worry, Tink. I have heard that word once or twice before. I want you to always be real with me, OK? ☺ ☺ ☺

Try to do some simple prayers for patience and God's love. I'll pray for you, too.

Fr. Rob

For stress reduct. long-term

1 — daily pray. ok keep brief — God prob. very busy.

2 — husb. for Little T.

3 — wife — Richard — not nun — nxt time togeth. tell him he's sick fuck.

Gaining insight into our hero's appetites (aka, Let Me Eat Cake).

MARGERY CASAWILL!
JOIN THE PARTY!
GRAND OPENING OF
MR. BBQ!
ENJOY A FREE SLICE OF MR. BBQ'S
WORLD FAMOUS
CHOCOLATE MOUSSE MOCHA CAKE
WITH ANY ENTRÉE!
TIME LIMITED OFFER

Beneath my anger at this postcard, I realize I am also salivating like one of Pavlov's dogs. Did they have to put a picture of that cake in full living color on the damned postcard?!? I should go get that freebie, in memory of my mother. She and I were no strangers to afternoon tea, brunches out, or any reason to eat good cake. Oh, she was always watching her diet. So she'd preface any treat, regularly, by saying, "I *never* do this." She was the Queen of Diet Rationalization. I learned well from her. Which is why I can't stop staring at the cake picture.

Cake and Mr. BBQ aside, let's face it: companies will do anything to sell their products. We're all a bunch of suckers. Shampoo

is *moisturizing*. Ice cream is *sinfully satisfying*. I still remember a yogurt ad a few years ago. Thirty-year-old slim gals walking along a beach eating yogurt…encouraging me to get my dairy products each day… saying it was part of a weight-loss plan…how did I know that eating eight of them a day would put on five pounds the first week?!

But labels and ads are not the only things that are deceiving.

Ben: Sweetheart, do you want to watch Earth's Nature Channel with me? It's about ostriches.

Me: Uh, maybe. I'll be down in a few minutes. How about putting some tea water on?

Ben: Already simmering on the stove, sweetie.

Is he wonderful or what? Although…he has seemed a little preoccupied. Almost distant the last few days. Maybe work pressures. I'd be concerned about "us," except that we're 100% totally in love. Maybe he scared himself, bringing up the marriage issue.

I go downstairs to join him on the sofa. The dog moves to the other side of Ben, sniffing and alert to any crumbs along the way. Ben is always the dog's person of choice, even though I raised him from a pup. Ungrateful.

Ben loves how beautifully photographed the nature shows on TV are. Earth's Nature Channel, though, could better be called "Watching Adorable Baby Animals Get Captured by Another Animal's Fangs." Every time, we get seduced by the loveliest, dearest little baby "Anythings" only to see the Mother Anything wander off for three seconds, and—here comes the Big Nasty Hungry Mean Animal, and then it's a race—the BNHMA has the Baby Anything flailing in its jaw-lock, while Mother Anything, back from window shopping, finally gets it that her babies are yummy to a larger species and she can't leave them alone without a sitter.

"Oh no, oh no, oh no!" I scream and cry at the TV. (And cling to Ben, which is very romantic even though I'm near-hysterical. Ben smells good. Sexy.)

"Oh, Ben! Oh, no!!!" as I half-shelter my eyes because I guess I also have a part of me that does need to see what's about to happen even though I know darn well what *will* happen. And Ben, ever the nature boy, just says, every time, "It's part of nature." No screams from him. He keeps on watching, ignoring my cries of "The babies! The babies!" and tries to point out that "The other animal is just trying to feed *her* babies so they don't starve."

"See?" he asks gently, "Aren't they cute, too?" and tries to get me to look at—well, OK—the most adorable little baby BNHMAs I've ever seen, who are now enjoying their very awful-looking meal.

Ben: By the way, your dad called earlier. Something about Bingo. I told him to triple his cards.

…patience…God's love…patience…

I hear Ben's phone ringing in another room.

"Your phone is ringing," I say, stating the obvious.

"I'll listen later. Don't worry about it," he says, and am I imagining he sounds a little edgy?

I'm on the way to bed when I hear, distantly, my phone ringing.

Ring. Ring. Beep. "Hi. It's Tink. Leave a message."

"Hi, Mom! It's Dylan! What's up? Yeah, well, I just wondered— do they still make those little low-fat cracker bits with peanut butter? And also, those good kind of pretzel nuggets? Yeah. Well, I think I'll go to the café. Getting kinda hungry. Love you, Mom!" *Click.*

Oh, gosh. I need to send him a little care package! He'll love that. I nursed that kid for a long time and I'll be darned if he's gonna go hungry now.

When I get to the bedroom, Ben is at his answering machine. I hear a decided *click* as I enter the room. What's going on?

"Oh, good, you're here!" he says, a little anxiously, "Let's go to bed."

Just what I was thinking.

{Chapter 18}

Katrinka fortifies herself with a therapeutic beverage prior to throwing herself to the bureaucratic wolves.

Did you know that at the drive-up window at some places the person talking to you can actually see you?! Turns out there's a little electronic eye on the menu sign. I heard that at some fast-food places, someone in another *state* sees you. Spooky. No more fingers where they shouldn't be on your face, no more obscene gestures, and no more mimicking the cheerful—or monotone—voice that comes through to take your order.

I am at one of my very-most-favorite-places-in-the-whole-world—Starbucks—and that's really saying something 'cause I have a lot of favorite places. It doesn't even matter that I'm already running late for work and I'll have to walk into the yearly benefits meeting in front of 40 people sitting in their little places listening to the usual sh—…well, anyway. I'm going to stop for my morning fix. I pull up to the drive-up window.

"I'd like an iced venti café mocha, two-thirds decaf, one-third caff, three pumps mocha, one percent, light whip with a teeny bit of drizzle, a long straw, and can I have a sleeve, please?"

Hahahahaha!!!! What kind of spoiled egocentric brat would actually order something like that?!?

Oh.

At the window, where I pick up my magnificent beverage on my way to my mundane hospital job (I mean, my exciting opportunity in the medical field to really make a difference in the lives of blah, blah, blah…), the sweet, dyed-black-haired, nose-ringed young woman takes my money as we wait for a new, confused-looking employee—oh, sorry, *barista*—to figure out how to make my complicated drink.

She: Almost ready! Then you can move on to your HAPPY DAY!"
Me: As good as it gets at the hospital where I work.
She: Oh. You're a nurse! Such an important calling.

She beams at me. Ah, youth. My brother would love her *(stop it stop it stop it!)* except she's no more than 30. *(STOP!)*
I look her straight in the eye.

Me: No, what *you're* doing is important work. I mean it. Nothing can happen of any importance without my coffee in the morning. I don't even need to drink it all. I just need to hold it and look at it in all its beauty. Now gimme. Before my boss gives me the hairy eyeball for being late again.

Hope I didn't cast a poor light on my profession.
These coffee friends understand me, and they're cheerful no matter what. They helped me through a slow transition to less fat and lower caff. They are the real heroes.
I leave the drive-up after a few more moments of chat and a lot of beeping horns coming from God knows where. People can be so touchy before their coffee.

At the office, we get four new e-mails about the Annual Safety Test. Of course, the hospital intranet is still down.

Ring. Ring. Ring. Static. Then, male auto-voice:
"You have reached the Help Desk. Please stay on the line and a

representative will be with you shortly. You are the…*fifty-third*…caller in line for assistance. Thank you for your patience." *Click.*

There's that damn word "patience" again. Wonder if Fr. Rob's really praying for me. Not that he doesn't have enough to do with masses, weddings, and fending off lonely single women.

I look at the growing stack of urgent messages next to my phone. How does that pile grow so much when my head is turned for, like, one minute? I'd love to find something to do that is fulfilling to me as a nurse. Something to turn the bureaucratic stuff into just a necessary nuisance instead of it being the main focus.

To: KatrinkaC@MeHosp.org
From: MyersE@MeHosp.org

Tink, I noticed you did not complete your Annual Safety Test last week.

Were you aware it was mandatory?…

(Oh, please, dear Lord.)

…You will still want to take it…

(No, I won't!)

…even though at this point it won't count toward your annual review and you told me it "has less importance than the number of flakes in my box of breakfast cereal on any given Monday morning." There will be other opportunities to gain points prior to your review by leading a Friday morning meeting or volunteering for the Best Practice Improvement Initiative Committee.

I'm frustrated by the new wave of hospital crap, but big business has changed things everywhere.

Once upon a time, our lives were simpler. Sleep, food, fitness. If you really couldn't sleep, maybe your doctor would toss a few sleeping pills your way. Now we are barraged with ads for sleep medications that are so seductive it makes everyone wonder if their sleep is up to par. TV cartoon-ads show rainbows and butterflies and pink hearts floating across a pale green sky.

Sleep peer pressure.

Patient: I only get eight hours of sleep at night. I need ten.

SHUT. UP.

Shit. I'd be happy with six. But the makers of certain new pills want us to think that we need their pill.

Patient: …the one with the moon and the stars…or is it the one with the Michelangelo painting?…or…

Oh—and your "health professional" will talk to you about "sleep hygiene." Who thought that one up?!? Sleep hygiene?!? Sounds like you smell bad.

We are told to lie down at the exact same time every night, to awaken at the exact same time, no TV in your room, no radio, no anything…holy shit. No wonder people can't sleep, with all those rules.

Sleep, fitness, stress, diet…I'm sick of hearing about the Northernmost Coast diet, the Eat-Like-Kids-Were-Starving-in-Korea-in-the-1950s diet, the Tape Your Mouth Shut diet…

Just a suggestion…a piece of chocolate INSTEAD OF THE WHOLE BAGFUL!!!

Oh, that reminds me.

pick up some snacks for Dylan — ? fruit roll-ups — healthy etc — send off in AM

Before I head out of the office, I try again to get onto the hospital intranet. Success!

And when I do, I see a notice announcing the Annual Nursing Competition. I've always wanted to do that. It involves one nurse from each department submitting a paper on an aspect of nursing care particular to his or her area. Think I'll talk to Gloria about volunteering. That could really bring back those good feelings about my work that I miss.

Maybe the tides are turning.

{CHAPTER 19}

In which our hero dabbles in being... "supportive."

~ *Impressions of Popcorn, Non-Buttered* ~
solo piece by L.T. Casawill
EAST END PARK
Li'l Punkin Daycare Theater
SUNDAY JUNE 1
8 p.m.
Donations gratefully accepted

Aunt Tink—Didn't get audition last wk.—but working p-t at a movie theater—great material for artistic expression!—Oh—and guess what? My agent got a bunch more auditions for me—keep your fingers crossed. So excited I can barely sleep! Maybe I should ask the Dr. about that little pill with the clouds and stars.

Seven thirty p.m.—the time when this princess starts turning into Crazy Mom, bundling up snacks for her son while dinner is cooking in the oven. Those homemade pork chop and baked potato smells tell me they're almost done. I'm starving. Again.

Quick e-mail to Little T, while it's still on my mind:

Sweetheart, your friend Dana wrote to me for advice.
Me. Imagine! Thing is—I really don't know where he can
find "exquisite ballet shoes the likes of which would
bring Baryshnikov to his knees" in NYC. Ideas?

What's this? Oh, no. No-no-no!

> **To: Tink@maine.com**
>
> **From: RealGuy@man.com**
>
> i am really lost—do U hear me??? lost! without my girlfriend. UR NOT helping.
>
> Gary

Yeah. Look, Gary, I'm trying to tape up a package to mail to my son. So suck it up.

Damn. Maybe I should just say that to him. Except it might not be what Fr. Rob meant about God's love and patience and all that.

Maybe this guy has no one else.

> **To: RealGuy@man.com**
>
> **From: Tink@maine.com**
>
> Gary, do not panic. I have a feeling it will be OK.
>
> Video games are a good distraction from your pain. Try that.
>
> "Aunt" Tink

Well, that was pretty lame, but it's all I got.

Don't let Little T meet anyone named GARY!!!

Ring. Ring. Beep. "It's Tink. It's Tink. Ugh. Leave a message."

"Hi, um, Aunt T? It's Little T. Um, I don't know a 'Dana.' Ahh, um, maybe he just kind of heard about you from one of my friends? Because they've all noticed how my auditions are going *much* smoother since I took your advice—to stick with it. Hmm…Dana…nope. No

Dana. Oh, hang on, Aunt — hey, are you guys going for coffee? Wait a sec! Gotta go, Aunt T. Mwwwwwaaaa!" *Click.*

> **To: Tink@maine.com**
> **From: Dylan@college.edu**
>   Hi, Mom! Quick note—forget the snacks—trying to
> lose a few pounds. But if possible, can you mail
> me my 10-pound weights? If you can. No hurry.
>   Love you—
>   Dylan

Sigh. I am sending those snacks. They're packed up and they're healthy, damn it.

The box of snacks, which were nearly pouring over, does my heart good. The box with the weights, which strain the cardboard to nearly breaking? Not so great.

After Ben and I have supper—way too much, but you know pork chops are just irresistible, especially the kind shaped like the letter P and cooked long enough to make the fat all crispy and…oh…uh, he goes into the other room and picks up his guitar. He looks so troubled, and I don't think it's because his cholesterol just soared to 1,000. I ask him what's going on. Turns out he saw a poster about guitar lessons at a music store and has been looking into it. He's embarrassed. Thinks he's too old to learn to play. That's where he was after work the other night, at their studio looking into it.

"That's so great!" I say, "Go ahead and have fun. I can just picture you and your guitar teacher forming a garage band!"

And he gives me this strange look.

Honestly!

{CHAPTER 20}

Struggling in earnest with one's Inner Grouch.

There's a long, long line inside the post office. I drag the bulging box of weights, along with the snacks, through the lobby, trying to grab packing tape and mailing supplies from the retail section as I make my way to the roped-off "Twilight Zone of Indefinite Waiting." Why do I always forget how crowded that place is?

After the post office stop, I fight the city traffic. I just hate it when people don't know what YIELD means, and it puts me on the verge of just—well, I begin my workday.

> **To: KatrinkaC@MeHosp.org**
>
> **From: MyersE@MeHosp.org**
>
> I was sorry to hear that you do not have time to be on the Improvement Committee.
>
> I've taken the liberty of nominating you for co-captain for the Annual Fund, just a great opportunity.
>
> By the way, I did get your Safety Test results, though I was surprised you didn't get a higher score. However, I was very pleased with your enthusiastic answers on the anonymous staff satisfaction survey.
>
> (*God, I am such a hypocrite. Then again—Annual Review.*)
>
> P.S.—Regarding your recent voicemail to me—please do not call me "honey." Respect Policy ☺

Through continuous paperwork and phone calls, meetings,

meetings, and meetings, I remind myself I am here for my wonderful patients. Oh, crap. The mandatory Financial and Psychological Considerations of the Medical Pharmacology New Age Forum in the Conference Room just started. I'm already late.

~ ~ ~ ~ ~ ~ ~ ~

Holy Mother of God!

I am so sick of hearing these words:

affirmation

empowerment

enlightenment

graph

healing

inner child (OK, that's two words)

grounded (not like "You're late—you're grounded!")

mindfulness

statistical

"from the get-go" (if I hear that one more time, someone is going to get seriously hurt)

journey

journaling (a noun morphed into a verb) and

respect

To these words, overused and misused, I have two of my own: SHUT. UP.

Thank God the damned meeting's over. Back to my desk to—

Oh, no. Today's also the mandatory Doctor-Nurse Mission Statement and Team Networking meeting.

vision

mission statement

evidenced-based (instead of making-shit-up medicine? Please. We're using leeches again.)

competencies

impact (as a verb…now, that just sounds nasty)

my sense is…

the trend seems to be…

the issues are…issues…issues…ISSUES!!!

"Little Dickie seems to be having some *issues* around structure." Duh! Little Dickie is FOUR MONTHS OLD!!!!

And so again,

SHUT. UP.

And fuck patience.

How's that for an affirmation?

To: KatrinkaC@MeHosp.org

From: MyersE@MeHosp.org

Does the fact that you haven't gotten back to me today regarding being our rep for the Annual Fund mean you'd rather do something else?

Buzz. Buzz. Beep. "You've reached the voicemail for Katrinka Casawill at the Outpatient Clinic. Please leave a detailed message and I will return your call. For the Prescription Refill Line, press four. For emergencies, press zero."

"Hi, Tink. Yeah, hi, it's Dr. D…"

Oh, great. The Helpless One.

"Just calling you for a little favor…"

Need help stirring your coffee?

"So—would you mind drafting up a letter for Mrs. Smithy about her cat? She has some issues with her landlord around keeping Puddles with her in her new place. Just make up something like

Puddles is a therapy cat and they can't be separated. That sounds good. Separation issues. That it would impact her health. That she has issues with separation and anxiety. And so does Mrs. Smithy. Ha-ha. Get it? Thanks, Tink—just take a stab at it, OK?"

It's not that I mind doing these little extra things for Dr. D. It's that he can't seem to get through his day without sucking the life out of me. I mean, he completely disintegrates if anything unexpected happens. Like a patient actually shows up.

> **To: KatrinkaC@MeHosp.org**
> **From: MyersE@MeHosp.org**
>
> Great! I'll sign you up to lead next Friday morning's staff meeting.
>
> P.S.—Not "sweetie," either. ☺

Fine. But I also have to do something more meaningful in my spare moments.

Oh, good. An e-mail from Dylan. He'll be so psyched when he gets the—

> **To: KatrinkaC@MeHosp.org**
> **From: Dylan@college.edu**
>
> Mom—know you're working—wanted to catch you. Do NOT need the 10-lb. weights—my friend has some he's not using. Gotta run—class in 10 min.—Love you!
>
> D.

{CHAPTER 21}

We pause, at this point, to allow our hero some further commentary on the state of the public restroom.

~ Stalling Tactics ~

I am back at the mall (I know. But it's just a quick stop) when I am forced to ask the profound question:

What kind of sadistic sicko bastard designed the standard public bathroom stall?

Each stall only allows someone who is 5'8" tall and 85 pounds to get in and out of said stall without either collapsing a lung or landing head first in the toilet bowl or the metal dirty-pad-collector on the wall thingie, which is always open with all its disgustingness poking out. They might as well forget the regular stall door and just put a little doggie in/out door at the floor level to crawl through.

~ ~ ~ ~ ~ ~ ~ ~

As I leave the mall restroom and head toward the parking lot, my mind wanders to the public bathrooms at work, where there are opened, usually damp rolls of toilet paper stacked behind each toilet—yuck!—lying in wait, in case the dispenser becomes empty. These commercial dispensers are so complicated, you'd need to call NASA to replace a roll. Once installed, it is scientifically impossible to get a free-flowing ribbon of TP. You're lucky to get one square at a time. Each try gets you just a thumbprint's worth of paper. You're pulling...then, *SNAP!* A shred of paper. Try again. *SNAP.* And *SNAP* and *SNAP* and

SNAP. Now you angle the paper as you ever-so-gently pull. Hey, this time you get a couple of inches. Progress. Then *SNAP!*

I must remember to talk to the uppers at work sometime about this situation. Our patients have enough problems without dealing with one-square-inch-only toilet paper dispensers. I mean, one of Dr. D.'s patients missed 15 minutes of his 20-minute appointment the other day due to an unexpected crap. The doctor's.

My cell phone is beeping. A message. Oh, it's Ben!

"Hi, Tink. Look, I'm still at the clinic. I have a lot of paperwork to finish. Didn't want you to worry about me 'cause I'll be a little late getting home. I love you."

Well, I'll catch up with him later. Hate to see him work such long hours.

As I drive home, I'm still thinking about those toilet paper dispensers at work. It's amazing how complicated some things are that don't need to be, like some public bathrooms that have double-decker toilet paper rolls inside the metal dispenser. You know, the kind that has a life force of its own. The top roll rests right on top of the bottom roll. I guess there's supposed to be a space between them. But there isn't. You see the end of the roll between them and pull. Suddenly, there are two lines of paper coming out from between them. The rule is, I think, to use the lower one first. Or is it the upper one. Well—you push the upper roll up an inch, holding it in place as you try to break off a decent-sized piece from the lower roll. Now, pull! One square. All this, and you're using both hands and you're all twisted off to the side. And you're holding up your skirt, or long sweater, or jacket at the same time.

And hovering.

You'd better be.

Didn't your mother warn you about toilets seats?!

p.u. hand/sanit. wipes @ groc. store—send
some to Dylan too—

{Chapter 22}

The beauty of a Crate & Barrel catalog, the kindness of a suitor, and a bout of long-overdue tears.

What a long day. I'm SO happy to be home, to put my feet up for a minute, have a little diet soda (I know all about its evils. Shut up.), have a little pre-supper cheese and crackers…luxury. Bad idea to go to the mall after work. Fridays at work are always rough. The usual stuff, plus eleven voicemails from family on my work phone, seven on my cell phone, all related to my parents' storage units, with vague offers of help and multiple pleas for items already packed into dozens of boxes marked "knick-knacks from living room," "knick-knacks from bedroom," "knick-knacks fr—," well, you get the idea. My generous mother could have fed all the children in the third world nations for what she and other well-meaning friends spent on knick-knacks and darling dishes over the years.

I look over today's mail.

****

MARGE CASAWILL!
HAVE A GREAT WEEKEND!
50% SAVINGS AT...

****

We spend the first half of our adult lives acquiring things and the second half trying to get rid of them and —

Oo-o-o—wait. Wait. What's this? *Yes!* The new Crate & Barrel catalog!

I'll just set that aside for later.

I open my bills and look them over carefully—twice—in the hopes that they've been miscalculated. I'll bet there's a mista— oh…they're correct. Ugh. How is it that four or five lunches out and a couple of trips to the mall could possibly add up to over $500? I put them back in the ever-growing pile of mail on the kitchen table and head upstairs to my computer, noticing that I'm being more and more pulled to that darned computer. Hope I'm not getting addicted. More important things in life. Simpler things, like nature, love, and—oh, wow!!

To: Tink@maine.com
From: BenL@MeHosp.org

Have you thought about the marriage idea? I sure do love you.

Ben

P.S.—I'll be home between 7 & 8 and I'll pick up some cold cuts. Don't worry about the storage units and all the family stuff. It'll all work out. You *really* don't need to take care of everything and everyone.

He's right. I forget how easily I get overinvolved in doing things. Step back…and refocus…on finding a nice young man for Little Tink, in case she comes up here to visit! And eventually, have a talk with myself and Ben about the marriage idea, which frankly scares me. I love him, but I've never been very successful at being married.

Wait. What's this…Crate & Barrel *online* special deals?!? Check. It. Out.

~ ~ ~ ~ ~ ~ ~ ~

In an amazing moment of relaxation, I have a cup of tea, and I'm reading a book. And bonus—Ben is unpacking the supper groceries. From another room, the phone rings, disrupting my personal R & R.

Ring. Ring. Beep. "It's Tink. It's Tink. Ugh. Leave a message."

"Oh. Ah…hi, Mom! It's Dylan! I was wondering—uh, can you mail me my New York Yankees sweatshirt? Also, I can't find an allowance check from a couple of months ago. Um, could you send me a replacement? I'm *pretty* sure I didn't cash it. Not this last check, the one before. Mom, your voicemail—uh, you sound a little stressed out. Are you OK? I love you, Mom. And tell Ben hi." *Click.*

I feel the tears coming. Hormones? Stress? Missing the kids? And my mom…

I have a good cry, not exactly sure of what I'm crying about, and then I feel a little better.

Think I'll change that outgoing message.

~ ~ ~ ~ *Reprieve* ~ ~ ~ ~

Let us pause briefly for our hero to have a short period of relative normalcy before the impending onslaught.

Yesterday was surprisingly calm and pleasant, a lazy kind of day for me and Ben. It's great to have a couple of those days in a row to really relax before the workweek begins. I even have a creative idea about the Annual Nursing Competition (the departmental nursing paper) to write about positive outcomes for people with chronic conditions through increased regular, supportive nursing "interventions" like phone calls. Can I sling the shit or what?!? Actually, it will take some hard work, but it's a subject I've thought about a lot in terms of patient progress. And I could really have some fun delving into it.

It's Sunday. A lovely Maine morning, sun shining. Ben and I have a great day planned—breakfast out, reading the Sunday paper, and singing in church with the folk group. And that's exactly how the day goes, for once. Almost makes me warm to the marriage idea. Which also makes me feel a little lightheaded, and I sense my pulse quicken.

And it's a little hard to get a deep breath.

{Chapter 23}

Katrinka is pulled in a plethora of directions.

Sunday evening.

Ring. Ring. Beep. "It's Tink. What's up?"

"Gwandma? It's Ewiott!!! Can you send me—what, Mommy? Huh? Um…uh…what, Daddy? Teapups?!? Hahahahahahaha!! Tea*pups*! Hahahahahahahaha!!!!! Mommy says teapups!!!!! Huh, Mommy? Dus videos? Oh, dus videos, Gwandma! Fast, Daddy? Telw—Gwandma—send—dem—vewy fast— Huh? Oh—*Pwease* send fast, I'm apposed ta say." *Click.*

Ring. Ring. Beep. "It's Tink. What's up?"

"Aunt T? It's Little T. I'm auditioning for the road tour of *Annie.* Again! Can you believe it?!"

Little Tink was in so many productions of Annie *as a kid, she started thinking she really was an orphan.*

"…Only this time it's for Mrs. Hannigan. At least it would be a paycheck. And don't worry, I'd have my cell phone and laptop with me—except show times—so we'd keep in touch. Mmmwahhh!" *Click.*

Ring. Ring. Beep. "It's Tink. What's up?"

"Tink? Gloria. Really sorry to call you at home. At least I didn't try you on the damn beeper. God! I fucking hate those things. Yeah—so—I'm in the middle of—well, never mind that—and the Boss beeps me. That went over big with the husband. Anyway, do you think you can go to the Pharmacy Review and Planning Committee meeting for me tomorrow? It's early—seven fifteen. In the morning. But I have an eight o'clock dentist's appointment I forgot about, fifteen miles away, and we really need someone there to represent the department. Thanks! I owe ya!" *Click.*

I listen to Ben strumming his guitar as I grab an apple to munch before I do some stretches and gentle floor exercise. Then—just the simple pleasure of winding down the evening, both of us reading in bed and getting sleepy.

Ring. Ring. Beep. "Hi. It's Tink. What's up?"

"Tiinnkkkk??? It's Dad. Dad. Your Dad. Ahh…ahh…it's Dad calling. Can you…oh…uh…I don't know where I put my slippers. Oh, damn. I guess you're not there. Well, call me back if you can. Wait. Wait a minute. Maybe those are my slippers over there under the… the…(silence) (*clunk*) (*thud*) Owwww!!!" *Click.*

Book down. Shoes on.

Crap. At least one of us gets to snore. I hear messages from the answering machine in the distance as I head downstairs.

Ring. Ring. Beep. "It's Tink. What's up?"

"Tink? Brenda from Gorgeous Ageless Gardens. Your Dad had a little accident. Bumped his head. Can you call us? I don't know if you want him to go to the ER. Or should we just watch him?" *Click.*

I'm grabbing my car keys to the tune of the final message of the evening.

Ring. Ring. Beep. "It's Tink. What's up?"

"Tink? It's Richard. Yeah. Look, if it would help you clear things out, I could use the white shower curtain from the downstairs bathroom the folks had at the condo, if you come across it in storage. Hey! I bet you thought I was calling you about getting me a date. Even though I thought your neighbor next door was very nice. *Very* nice. Anyway, no teacups, Tink! But, see if you can find the…"

It's 11:30 p.m. as I leave the house. The quiet night has a clean, forest smell. Maybe no one will notice I'm wearing my PJs under my coat.

~ ~ ~ ~ ~ ~ ~ ~

My beeper is going off.

I use the nearby ER bedside phone.

Me: What?!

Dr. Myers: Oh, ah, sorry, Tink. Couldn't sleep. Thought I'd try out the system during the night shift…Hello? Hello? Tink?

…patience…love…peace…

Me: Give me *your* beeper number. In case I have to call YOU some night.

Dr. Myers: Gee, Tink, I will, but you know we're just doing this as a patient safety issue. You know, it's a darned good Quality Improvement project. Ah—are you on that committee?

I finally get home at 3 a.m. My answering machine is blinking from an earlier message.

"Mom, it's Dylan. What's up? Hey, don't send me the sweatshirt. I'm coming home for a weekend at the end of the month. Got a ride. And hey—thanks for the snacks. They're awesome! Well, can't wait to see you guys. Love you!" *Click.*

Glad he's coming home. Glad I waited before sending the sweatshirt.

My Dad's safely back at Gorgeous Ageless Gardens. All is well.

I go to bed and drift off for the remaining three hours of the night, reassuring myself that things will most assuredly get easier soon.

{Chapter 24}

In which our hero finds out that just when she thinks things can't get any worse...comes the crash.

Monday. 7 a.m.

I'm driving to the damn Pharmacy Review and Planning Blah Blah Bullshit Committee meeting. The sun is barely up. And I think...I'm getting cramps. Already? At this rate, I could try for the Guinness Book.

Uh-oh. My cell phone is ringing.

Breathe in the light...release the stress...breathe in the—

I'm pulling into the hospital parking lot as I check the message:

"Tink? Hello! It's Brigid in Holland!"

Brigid? Wow. I haven't heard from her in months. She's a long-time family friend.

"I'm sorry I do not call sooner. I hope you very well now. I think of you many times since your mother die. Um, Tink...I find out she have teacup collection, very nice as I like teacup for tea in each morning. Maybe you send me one. A pretty one, yes? With some nice color on it, too? Well, bye-bye now!"

...release the stress...

~ ~ ~ ~ ~ ~ ~ ~

The morning drones on with an arrhythmia of computer and phone noise, doors opening and closing, patient and physician voices, and occasional shouts of "Damn computer!!" coming from the nearby offices.

> **To: KatrinkaC@MeHosp.org**
>
> **From: MyersE@MeHosp.org**
>
> Tink, I noted that you attended the Pharmacy Committee meeting this morning. Thank you. I am, however, a little puzzled as to how you were able to add that on to your "freaking ridiculous slave girl workload."

Isn't it time for him to be pulling his room-temperature cheese sandwich out of his paper lunch bag?

I send off a quick e-mail to Gloria to let her know I'm volunteering to write the nursing paper for the Annual Nursing Competition, explaining my idea for it.

"AWESOME!!" she flies back. "And thank you SOOOO much!"

There. That feels great. And meaningful. It will be a lot of research, but right from my nursing heart. In fact, it—

Wait. What?!?

> **To: KatrinkaC@MeHosp.org**
>
> **From: RealGuy@man.com**
>
> so, Tink Casawill—if that's your real name—i hear you're a nurse—very impressive. what's NOT impressive? my girlfriend Annie—no, my *ex*-girlfriend—still hates me. how do you live with yourself?!? i deserve better than this, you moron advice-giver. can't even sleep.
>
> Gary

Damn.

To: RealGuy@man.com
From: KatrinkaC@MeHosp.org

How did you get my work e-mail address?!? I'm not allowed to do this on company time. If you must write, use my other e-mail. Or let Annie know how you feel…

(Maybe that will help. I know he sounds obnoxious. But—you know—happy ending.)

…and try warm milk before bed for sleep.

I pause to consider how annoyed I'm getting with so many things, and then I look up at my bulletin board littered with pictures of family at various ages, bringing back happy memories, seeing some of them in a different light, as though for the first time, noticing how very pretty and sweet-looking my mom was, and how cute and chubby Dylan was as a toddler.

And suddenly, a harsh sadness overtakes me. My kids grown, my mom gone…Oh, no. I don't want to cry here, at my desk, with people popping in and out of my office as if it were a train station lobby.

~ ~ ~ ~ ~ ~ ~ ~

To: KatrinkaC@MeHosp.org
From: BenL@MeHosp.org

Hey, girlfriend—want to go out for lunch? Can you get away for an hour for some Chinese food? Love you!

An hour away from work? Lunch out?

Yes. Just what the doctor ordered.

Not Even Dark Chocolate Can Fix This Mess

Oh, this was not the type of midday break I had in mind.

1:03 p.m.
Note to Idiot Driver:
RED LIGHT = STOP!

YOU.
BIG.
ASSHOLE!!!!

And so our hero, as often happens in such tales, has encountered a dragon—in the form of a ton of metal. We follow her as she makes her way through the pain of her encounter, the beginning of her recovery via the medical persons of the day, a simple amusement called the television, and the added joy of being female.

Ouch.

I've got cold packs on various body parts, medication at hand, popcorn, a pint of Häagen-Dazs, and the ever-comforting television. Ben is next to me on the sofa being, um, supportive.

~ ~ ~ ~ ~ ~ ~ ~ ~

Early the next morning, very slowly, I get out of bed. Couldn't sleep, sore all over. Ben is sleeping as I attempt to get dressed. I am still reeling from the shock and terror of seeing something very large ram into my formerly nice little vehicle, with me in it. It's all I could think about during the night. Ben held me—very, very carefully—as I cried and shouted and cried some more, and I have a feeling it's going to be a long time before I don't jump at unexpected sounds. Or before I can stop clutching the dashboard, as I did after the accident when Ben drove me to the "Urgent Care" doctor and then home.

The ambulance at the scene had offered me a ride to our hospital's ER and no thank you, I will not be waiting in a crowded crappy ER with a bunch of people coughing and puking, crying babies, intoxicated teenagers post-fistfight, the place teeming with germs, noise, sweat, bad air, dozens of questions being asked over and over, waiting for insurance to clear—*no*.

~ ~ ~ ~ ~ ~ ~ ~

Ben—
Thanks for making all those insurance calls for me.
I'll be home in a few hours—after the MRI. Am really, really nervous about going into that thing. Sounds like a fucking coffin. BTW, can you please call my brother, maybe Lorraine, and anyone else in the family you think should know what happened? They're going to have to help more now, sorting through stuff at Dad's storage units. We have to clear them out as soon as possible—rental $$.
Love. —T.
P.S.—Thanks—ice cream. Yes—marry—later. Too much now.
P.P.S.—Can you stop at the drugstore after work and get me tampons (<u>medium, unscented</u>) & pads (<u>medium, chlorine-free</u>, & <u>NO WINGS</u>)?
P.P.P.S.—Use coupons on table (ones in my <u>mother's</u> name. <u>HA</u>!)
P.P.P.P.S.—Ouch.

~ ~ ~ ~ ~ ~ ~ ~

Buzz. Buzz. Beep. "You've reached the voicemail for Dr. Lambert at the Medical Clinic. Please leave a message and I will return your call as soon as possible. For emergencies, please press zero and await further options."

"Hi. Um, am I calling the right number for 'Ben?' This is Sandra calling from the Imaging Center, 555-0189. Just calling to say you'll need to pick up your, um—wait—what did she say?…oh, yeah—your *'Arabian Mistress of* —ahem—*Sexual Delight'*—at our MRI area. *Barb, quick! Help her! She's trying to get up!!* Sorry about that. We, uh, had to give her a wee bit of valium to get the MRI done. Actually, a bunch of wee bits of valium. You know, claustrophobia. Dr. Alfred said to tell you she has injury to her neck and back and wants to see her in his office tomorrow at noon to examine her again and go over treatment options. Please call back. And have a great day!" *Click.*

~ ~ ~ ~ ~ ~ ~ ~

The next morning, I awaken, hopeful, only to find I feel even worse. Nevertheless, I ever-so-gingerly get ready for work, and crank up Ben's old Honda Civic, which still holds its own after more than 10 years.

I pass Gloria's office, and hover in her doorway so I can let her know I'll have to leave at lunchtime for a follow-up doctor's appointment. That's when I catch:

"…awful about your accident! I feel so bad for you. But listen, take all the time you need and just get bet—"

I hobble over to the chair next to her.

"Tink? WHAT ARE YOU DOING HERE?!?"

I am actually asking myself the same question. What happened to my pledge to take care of myself? If I had any sense, I'd pack a small suitcase and go lie on a warm beach somewhere for a few weeks. Talk about your healing thoughts...

~ ~ ~ ~ ~ ~ ~ ~

Home again, home again, jiggedy-jig.

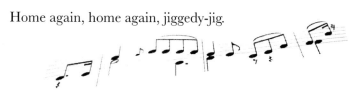

I comfort myself with ice cream. And popcorn and seltzer. And reruns of *The Golden Girls* on TV. My sofa is full of me, ice packs, and pillows.

Ring. Ring. Beep. "It's Tink. (*Ouch.*) Leave your message."

"Hi. Dr. Alfred's office calling, following up. We're going to set up physical therapy in the next few weeks. He said let's give the soft tissue time to calm down before the treatment starts, so keep up your cold packs and the things the doctor told you about. Your PT will be at St. Regina's Hospital Outpatient Department down in York County. Couldn't get you in at your hospital. Sorry. If you hop on the Turnpike, it should only take you about forty-five minutes to get there. Hope that won't be too hard on you." *Click.*

South. But not exactly a faraway beach location.

To: FrRob@StPeter.org
From: BenMan@maine.com

Hi, Father Rob.

Special request from Tink—can you please increase prayers? Patience is taking a backseat (no pun intended) to the pain of getting crashed

into at an intersection. Injured, not life-
threatening. Hoping for a quick recovery. Tink
says maybe you could do the praying for her?

    Ben

Ring. Ring. Beep. "It's Tink. (*Ouch.*) Leave your message."

"Hey—it's Gloria. *Of course* you need to go to your appointments. Use sick time. Or vacation time. Hey, maybe catch up on some reading!" *Click.*

~ ~ ~ ~ ~ ~ ~ ~

DID I NOT SAY <u>NO</u> <u>WINGS</u>?!?

I really can't get mad at him. He's SO good to me.

But I just hate those damned wings. Not only are they useless (follow my reasoning here for a minute: if you're, uh, flowing enough to leak beyond a no-wing pad, won't you still leak beyond a winged pad, just an inch or so over from there? I mean, is it really gonna help?), but also, what the hell do you do with the 3/4"x 3/8"oblong pieces of waxed paper that come off the wings, and if you can manage to pull said papers off, how often does the whole thing fall into place and not get all twisted up on itself? God.

~ ~ ~ ~ ~ ~ ~ ~

What is it with the little people and ads at the bottom of the TV screen?!?!

I'm trying to distract myself with a little TV while doing comfort measures. In the middle of the most dramatic part of *House*, I have to see a half-dressed, bearded wrestler in miniature fooling around at the bottom of the screen, or a preview of the next show coming up completely ruining the moment when House and Cameron are looking intently at each other. He's leaning in, and then a WWF idiot's making hand signals. WHY?!? Makes me want to go screaming from the room.

But I don't. I'm "recuperating." I hurt, and OK, maybe I'm a little hormonal.

Prior to today, I enjoyed a few TV shows with Ben. *Law and Order. South Park. Curb Your Enthusiasm.* And occasionally, the news, where one can get a glimpse of how truly stupid some people are. I mean the newscasters who think they have to entertain us. Just give us the damned news.

Ring. Ring. Beep. "It's Tink. *(Ouch.)* Leave your message."

"(giggle) It's Ewiott again, Gwandma! Teapups? Hahahahaha haha!!! Tea PUPS!!!!!!!!!!!!!!! Hahahahahahaha!!!!!!! Mommy wants the wed one, too. Hahahaha!!!!! What, Daddy? Not wed? White and wed? Huh, Daddy? You want me to telw Gwandma…huh? Wait a minute, Gwandma. Daddy, awe you in the bafwoom now? Gwandma, Daddy's in the potty now. Poopie! HAHAHAHAHA!! Poopie! What, Katie? I'm not apposed to say *what*?" *Click.*

Aw! He's so dear. I wish my little grandchildren lived nearby. I know being with them would soothe my aching self.

I readjust the cold pack. I just hate dealing with all my medical stuff, not only at appointments at various offices, but lots at home—the heating pads, the cold packs, balms, pillows, rolled-up towels, tennis balls…tennis balls? Don't ask.

```
To: Tink@maine.com
From: FrRob@StPeter.org
```

Tink, got you in my prayers. Me, and 23 other priests and brothers here at the "compound." We got ya covered. ☺

Love,

Fr. Rob

~ ~ ~ ~ ~ ~ ~ ~

The home treatments are so BORING, I could go insane. I'm watching too much TV now while I do them, including a lot of specials that deal with health. And I have time, more time than I've had in a long time, to think. And not just about matchmaking, either. I'm seriously going to give that up. After Little Tink and my brother each find true love.

No, I'm thinking mostly about my mom. She used to tell me so many things about her life—her childhood during the Depression, the songs of her day (complete with her smiling soprano voice, shakier in her later years), what it was like during WW II, rationing for food. I'd tease her: "Oh, this sounds like Epic Number 438" and she'd giggle. I loved hearing those stories over and over again. It's been just a few months since her death, and some of her accounts are already fading from my memory.

I think about my poor dad, living without her, and how lonely it must feel to him.

If only…if only I could talk with my mom now. She'd be here helping me, bringing me good deli food, homemade chicken soup, and cheering me up and saying, "Aww—poor Tink." She'd even be bringing me special silly reading material I like. As a child, she'd supply me with new coloring books and crayons when I wasn't feeling well (talk about your positive reinforcement for being sick!) and I think I'm pretty well past the coloring books. But I still enjoy a good *Betty and Veronica* comic book now and then. A stress reliever for a few minutes, it helps me set aside the so-called important stuff, like mounting piles of paperwork. They can wait a little longer. I have to save my energy for getting better and being moody. That takes a lot of work.

Don't forget—re Little T—chat up nice
pharmacist—ask re pain med or anything—find
out if gay—if has Sig. other—etc. etc.

Ring. Ring. Beep. "It's Tink. (*Ouch.*) Leave your message."

"Hello, Tink. Hannah from Dr. Alfred's office. Turns out St. Regina's isn't a preferred provider for your insurance coverage, but we'll see what we can set up somewhere else. Let's just say if you don't hear otherwise, we'll find another physical therapy group and have them contact you directly. Have a great day."

{Chapter 26}

A televised pharmaceutical ad launches our slightly unstable hero toward the edge of temporary insanity.

The bad part of being home is the television set. Ads that tell us how new medications will solve everything from sexual dysfunction to mental fatigue to heartburn, getting people all excited about a cure, only to list side effects not even Superman could endure. I mean, watery stools? Is any pill worth that?

Then there's the news. "Latest findings" indicate there is nothing safe to eat anymore.

12:00 News:

"Can that salad cause a life-threatening illness that lands you in the hospital? And what about the safety of prepared supermarket meals? More tonight, on a special six o'clock news report: 'Outrage on Your Dinner Plate!' Join our news team…"

I look down at the big bowl of crunchy green stuff in front of me, half-eaten. And set it aside. Thank God there are chips in the house.

Occasionally on the news, I hear about medical breakthroughs. Here is one that everyone should know about. It can affect millions. And you read it here first. From Aunt Tink to *you*:

**** BREAKING MEDICAL NEWS ****
**** BREAKING MEDICAL NEWS ****
REPEAT : BREAKING MEDICAL NEWS!!!!!

"FRS"

There is a medical condition rampant in this country that no one talks about. I am referring to "FRS." For those of you "out of the loop" (which is like a fucking crime nowadays—you gotta stay "in the loop!" Just what does this loop look like, anyway, and what's it made of? What if I choose to stay "to the side of the loop?" You can't, because everyone wants to keep you "*in* the loop." Just once, for one whole day, I'd like everyone to shut up about the damned loop.)

I'll start that sentence again.

So—for those of you out of the loop, FRS stands for Fart Retention Syndrome, a serious and increasingly common ailment in the adult population, worsened by the influx of the female workforce over the last several decades and by the rising age of retirement. I know what you're thinking: males would never fall victim to this…

Oh—Ben's home!

"Hi, honey. Brought home a cooked chicken from the supermarket and a big salad from the salad bar!"

At work, I share an office with a wonderful and unflappable nurse, Peggy. I've nicknamed her Unflappable Peg. For the majority of each day, we are sitting nine feet, three and a half inches apart, give or take, depending on if one of us is leaning back or swiveling in her chair.

What is wrong with you? you may wonder. *You're actually measuring the distance?*

Ah. One of the early signs of FRS.

Medically speaking, it is known as Casawill's FRS, named after me because that's what we scientists do when we discover something. Look, it could be worse. Take, for example, Benjamin Landow Bergdorf, who named Bergdorf's Prolific Pinna Male Hirsutism after himself—the phenomenon of a boatload of hair growing out the ears of old men. OK, I made that up. But anyway, when FRS lands in the real medical journals, I want my name attached to it.

What exactly *is* this ailment, FRS? I think it speaks—or doesn't speak—for itself. The most common characteristics of the syndrome include: gas buildup, in varying amounts, not released in a timely manner during a normal eight-hour workday; said gases build up not because of abnormal body structure or disease, but due to inaccessibility of a private space and/or the overwhelming demands of a job that keeps one at her desk for long periods of time while in the nearby proximity of a coworker, patient, or customer for whom one has a heart. This excess gas causes bloat and crankiness and, now that I really think it through scientifically, weight gain. Yeah, that's it. Weight gain.

I've settled into a comfy chair, heating pad behind me, pillows under each arm, as I write about FRS.

"Tink. Haven't you been on that heating pad for fifteen minutes already?"

"Yeah. But I'm in the middle of an important scientific discovery."

"Want me to get the cold pack?"

"No, honey, not yet. Thanks."

"I love you, babe."

"I love you more."

{*Chapter 26*}

He looks less stressed-out tonight. Good.

I know I have personally experienced severe bouts of FRS.

My office mate, well-meaning, has in the past given me the go-ahead to relieve my symptoms:

"Don't worry about it. Really," Peggy says.

Right.

Many, many years ago my mother was at an exclusive restaurant in New York City. She needed to use the restroom. While she was there, in walked a lovely, elegantly dressed woman in her mid-thirties. As my mother reapplied her bright red lipstick, she overheard the other woman, from a distant stall, gently announce:

"Pardon me, ladies, but I need to fart."

Our family's favorite story ever.

I would *never* announce such a thing. I simply retain. And retain. And retain.

And then, the blessed moment arrives: my office mate gets called to another room, or goes to the copy machine down the hallway.

At last—alone.

I take a peek into the hallway, and shut my door.

…Relief…

And then, every single time, like a MAGNET, in comes a member of my team—or my boss. To ask me a question. I mean EVERY. TIME.

But let me back up.

I wear a phone headset. So when that unsuspecting visitor walks in, I quickly hold out my right arm, like "Wait! Stop there!" while pointing to my headset with the forefinger on my left hand. SO THEY WILL THINK I'M ON THE PHONE—YET THEY KEEP COMING UNTIL THEY'RE ACTUALLY HOVERING OVER ME LIKE MY FREAKING GUARDIAN ANGEL. What is it with these people? Can I not have two seconds of peace? Oddly, no one ever says anything like, "Whoa! Something die in here?" I don't get it. Have they completely lost their olfactory sense?

Ben walks through our TV room carrying his guitar.

"Tink. Did you fart? It really smells bad in here."

"No, Ben. I did not. Maybe it was the dog."

"Oh. OK. Love you."

Phew.

Must remember to give that dog a treat.

FRS continued…

Just for the record, I try to do this differently. I try to lock my office door, which doesn't work anyway because we all have master keys. And sometimes, I even make it to the gross staff bathroom before, you know, letting go. Except it is immediately next to the patient waiting room. Who planned that one?!

Further research that I've imagined shows that children, with their increasingly busy schedules, are also prone to Juvenile FRS, due to fewer recesses at school…talk about your childhood obesity epidemic! All gas.

Somewhere between birth and kindergarten age, we become aware of holding in air. But that has to change. I took a long walk yesterday and tooted the whole way. Lost eight pounds. Just like that.

{CHAPTER 27}

Katrinka begins to experience mounting external demands, and longs for comfort and security.

In theory, working part-time while I tend to my injury should be workable. But any time you read those words—"in theory"—you know it's crap.

I'm getting ready to leave my office, pocketbook in hand, when I hear my work phone ring.

Buzz. Buzz. Beep. "Hi. Nurse Tink will be out for the rest of the day. For the Prescription Refill line, press four. To reach another nurse or for emergencies, press zero."

Not everyone gets it. How much clearer do I need to be?

"Tink, Dr. D. here. Uh, I wondered if you could come help me with a patient who needs to get set up for a non-urgent CT scan. I could send her in to your office to—wha—? Oh. Huh? Oh, I didn't realize— never mind, Tink. Gloria just told me you had (cough, sputter)—sorry, Tink, cough drop mishap…(cough)…ahem…a medical appointment to go to. I guess maybe I could…well…I'm kinda late for lunch. Actually, I have other things for you to do for me. Not sure how badly you got hurt. Oh, wait. Pretty bad, huh, Gloria? Well, I'll just leave the stuff in your mailbox. Hope you can get to them kinda soon. You know. If you can. As a favor? Yeah. That's it. A favor." *Click.*

Driving home, I realize how pressured I feel to get my work done in a shortened day…starting the department nursing paper… keeping up with my treatments…the pain itself…and all the tasks to attend to at home. It's too much. I need to pull back and prioritize. Prioritize? Ugh. I'm beginning to sound like management.

~ ~ ~ ~ ~ ~ ~ ~

~REFLECTIONS FROM THE SISTERS OF OUR MOST PRECIOUS LORD~
DEAR ASSOCIATES OF THE SISTERS OF OUR MOST PRECIOUS LORD, AS YOU ARE AWARE, WE ARE UNDERGOING MANY CHANGES AS WE CONTINUE ON OUR JOURNEY. PLEASE READ THE ENCLOSED—A RICH TEN PAGES!—AND CAREFULLY CONSIDER THE OPTIONS BEFORE US. WE LOOK FORWARD TO A SERIES OF MEETINGS, WHICH WE HOPE YOU WILL BE ABLE TO ATTEND. YOURS IN OUR PRECIOUS LORD, SISTER MARY HOWARD

Feeling guilty, I drop the ten pages of half-crumpled paper into the trash can.

The irony is I could really use the connection with this group right now. I just don't have the extra minutes.

> To: FrRob@StPeter.org
> From: Tink@maine.com
>
> Fr. Rob,
> Do priests send out massive mailings like the Sisters do?
> Just wondering.
> —Tink

To: Tink@maine.com
From: FrRob@StPeter.org

Tink,

No. It is unreal, isn't it? One time I was
asked to proofread a series of their mailings. I
thought I was going to have to hang myself, and as
you know, that is against our religion.

We're guys here. Few words.

Plus, a few of us are so old we're lucky we can
breathe, much less write.

Always,

Fr. Rob

Ben offers to send out a family e-mail.

"Hi, everyone! For those who didn't hear, Tink is a bit banged-up from the recent accident, so please give her time to recover. We really have our hands full right now. Thanks for your understanding. —Ben"

Then he goes off, and I think I hear him making a call from his other phone, downstairs. Probably calling one of his old friends. It doesn't matter who he's calling. We're our own people.

Who's he calling?

Just then, my phone starts ringing.

Ring. Ring. Beep. "It's Ben. Tink is resting. Leave a message."

"Hi, Tink. It's Richard. Sorry to hear you got hurt! Guess this means I won't meet your friend tomorrow night at the steak place? Should we meet without you? Call me, OK? 'Cause if we don't go out, I might go to Boston instead, or the stock car races. Or maybe you need me to come help you with some chores or something?" *Click.*

Oh, no! Please, please don't. He's so dear, but, well, he's not all that helpful and it usually ends up being more work or expense for me. Like the time he was visiting and we had a big ice storm. He stayed overnight and the next morning, he was out on our deck chopping away some built-up ice. To help us. Accidentally swinging the ax through our new $3,000 deck. He meant well.

Ring. Ring. Beep. "It's Ben. Tink is resting. Leave a message."

"Hi, Aunt T! It's Little T—on tour. I hear someone totaled your car. Are you OK, Aunt T? Oh—I *hope* you don't mind—a few days ago, I "Pro-Blogged" you—'cause so many of my show biz friends wanted to be able to chat with you—Um…do you know how to get into a blog? Just log on to www.AskAuntTink.com and, uh, hope you don't mind I put a picture of you on it. And some cute designs on the front page—check it out! Yeah—and my head shot with audio of me singing a Broadway-type Gospel song. Just in case. You know—free publicity. So, call me and I'll tell you how to get onto your blog if you're stuck. Love you! Get better fast!" *Click.*

What?!? I know she trusts me, and that's really sweet and flattering, but now I have to be *everyone's* auntie? Of course, she didn't know what was going on with me. Well, I'll just put that on hold. Until I feel better.

If not pharm. √ into nice resid.

@ hosp. for Little T—husb. to rely on!

{*Chapter 27*}

Ring. Ring. Beep. "It's Ben. Tink is resting. Leave a message."

"Tink? It's Lorraine. Are you OK? I'm worried about you. I was planning on coming up this weekend and helping you go through the things at the storage units. Should I still come up? You know, I could help get things sorted. I'll just stay with you guys, OK? And bring my own sheets. Tink—do you think you could pick up some grapefruit and organic apples at the store in case I get up there late and the stores are closed? I'll pay you back, so don't worry about that. Oh, and some granola. Low fat. Organic. You know, I'm doing this special nutrition program—really good. You should try it. Also, do you have any whole-grain crackers? Could you pick up a box of them? I think you know the brand I like. It starts with a T. Oh—maybe it's an R. Or a K. Well anyway, get the 'Originals.' Call me back. And look, if you can't get to the store, don't sweat it—I'll just come up anyway and help out." *Click.*

Ring. Ring. Beep. "It's Ben. Tink is resting. Leave a message."

"Tink, it's Adeline. Honey, are you OK? Do you need help getting to doctor's appointments? I'm very worried about you, sweetheart." *Click.*

Weird.
Adeline always seems to know when I need to hear from her.
Oh.
I get it.

Ring. Ring. Beep. "It's Ben. Tink is resting. Leave a message."

"Hi, Mom! It's Ali. I'm so sorry about the accident! Are you OK? That's so sad and scary. John says he hopes you've had a specialist look at you. Oh, hey—I heard you had a blog! How'd you figure that one out?…Katie! 'Figure': F-I- then what? Huh? Good. Oh, sorry, Mom. Yeah, about the blog. No offense, but last I knew you could barely type. Wait. Elliott wants to play 'Twinkle Twinkle' for you on his violin, don't you, Elliott? That'll help you feel better, Mom. Elliott? Elliott!! ELLIOTTTTT! PUT THAT DOWN AND GO GET YOUR VIOLIN SO GRANDMA CAN—Oh, no! NO! That *damned dog*! Oh, crap. I have to go. He just—DON'T STEP IN IT, ELLIOTT! UGH!" *Click.*

Ring. Ring. Beep. "It's Ben. Tink is resting. Leave a message."
I hear a husky voice.

"Uh, hello. Is this the right number for Tink's *Aunt* Tink? Uh, Tink said I could call for a little support. If I couldn't wait for an answer online. See, my girlfriend left me last week and I'm pretty upset. If you could call me back, Aunt Tink, that would be really good. My number is 555-0177. Thanks. Call me, OK? I'll be up 'til midnight, at least. Oh, yeah, ask for Estelle." *Click.*

Oh. OK. I'm hip.
Having heard enough voicemails, I start checking my e-mails.

> **To: Tink@maine.com**
> **From: BenMan@maine.com**
>
> Hey, I'm sitting behind you, baby. Can I have a moment of your time tonight? Just want to tell you about the guitar lessons I set up. And to snuggle you.

Ben and I have our computers side to back, about four feet apart in the computer/guest room. And I read this e-mail and turn around, as best as I can since the accident, and he is looking at me with that look that makes my heart just—

Ring. Ring. Beep. "It's Ben. Tink is resting. Leave a message."

"Tink? Lorraine. Um, could you also pick up some vanilla soy milk, if you get to the store? Thanks. Hope it's not too much trouble. Thank you SO much. Love you! Oh—also, I need directions to your house." *Click.*

Oh, come on. *Every* time she needs directions? I'm getting her a GPS for her next birthday.

I slowly turn back toward Ben, who is now burning his eyes into m—

Ring. Ring. Beep. "It's Ben. Tink is resting. Leave a message."

"Hi, Mom! It's Dylan. Just wondered—when I come home at the end of the month, would it be OK to bring my girlfriend?…"

(*Oh, good! I really like her and it's so cute to see them together!*)

"…And also my roommate…"

(*Uh, well, OK. Sure, that'll be —*)

`"…and his cousin who's visiting from France. Is that OK, Mom?"

(*Sigh. What we do to spend, oh, maybe 12 or 13 minutes out of a weekend with our precious college kids?*)

I pick up the phone.

"Hi, honey…"

~ ~ ~ ~ ~ ~ ~ ~

When I look back, Ben is busy playing Solitaire on his computer.

Might as well check out this blog thing while I have a moment of near-comfort.

WHAT?!?

Well, there probably won't be this many letters all the time. And I suppose I could answer just one or two. After all, a lot of these people might not have anyone to talk to. Kind of my way to "give back." Or whatever that deal was when I signed on to be an Associate.

Ask Aunt Tink

Personal Advice for Your Personal Problems!

post a question | review account | emails recieved 43

Hi, everyone! Wow, I see there are a shitload of—

No, wait—Delete—start again.

Hi, everyone! Wow, I see there are quite a few of you! Phew! Aunt Tink has had a long day. It may take some time to answer everyone. Feel free to answer each other as you wish, OK? I'm pretty sure there's a way to do that. Just click around a little.

But for now, let me just tell you—and I think you know who you are—that today and tonight you should treat yourself very, very nicely. Do something healthy and soothing for yourself. A cup of tea. A good book. A piece of fruit. An old movie. See if that helps with your problem.

Special note to "On the Edge"—Don't jump. I don't think it's even legal. I understand you have "disappointment issues," but truly, your bookstore could probably order the new CD you want. Or try online or something. You may need to ask your "inner child" to knock it off and be patient.

{*Chapter 27*}

One last thing to EVERYONE:
About that piece of fruit—Always wash your fruits
and vegetables well!

Ouch.

Have to go to bed. Tomorrow will be easier—will feel better after good night's sleep.

"Ben?" I ask, and turn towards…his empty computer chair. Damn. I just lose track of time.

He's in bed, asleep, so I sneak in and snuggle up next to him and enjoy his snoring and figure I'll hear about the guitar lesson details tomorrow. He grunts and throws an arm over me. I move in closer until he readjusts his position. I feel so safe in his arms, and I close my eyes.

{Chapter 28}

Although not a medieval court jester, our hero performs a modern-day juggling act.

You know the muscles that go between your shoulders and your neck? On both sides? And the ones that go up the back of your neck into your scalp? And the big long ones that go down both sides of your spine? And all the little and middle and larger ones that surround your ribcage, front and back? Well, they hurt. They hurt enough to make me feel queasy in the stomach. They are rock-hard to the touch, and so sore I can barely stand the clothing on them.

I am at work, juggling every hot pack and cold pack I can get my hands on, in various achy parts of my anatomy, while catching up on voicemails from several doctors and social workers on my team. I am not happy.

And a certain Dr. D. just doesn't get that he's not the only one with needs.

"Hi, Tink—it's Dr. D. Hey—no big hurry, but can you schedule an EKG for Mrs. Rushmore? For tomorrow? Also, I'll need her labs from her primary care doc. Oh—I should have had her sign a release. Uh, can you call her and kind of figure that out? Before tomorrow?..."

(*Silence, followed by crackling noise—ah—taking out a lozenge.*)

"...That would just be an incredible favor—really peachy-keen. Oh, also, can you do the eight-page initial treatment plan on this morning's intake? Oops—I think I already sent my notes down to Medical Records. Well, maybe..."

(*OK. Not only is Dr. Incompetent completely dependent on everyone around him and a scared weenie, but must he use language like he just walked out of a really bad 1960s sitcom? Just once, I'd like to hear something PG-13 out of him. God.)*

"…I hate to ask you to do my work…"

(*Uh-huh…*)

"…but I have a couple of important meetings at HR and I really, really need to set up a retirement account for myself. I mean, I'm almost thirty-two. Can never start too soon, right? Heh-heh. Oh—also, we need…"

(*Z-z-z-z-z-z…*)

"…forwarding a bunch of patient calls to you. Let me know if I need to do anything about them. Thanks. Oh—hey, golly—hope you're feeling better!" *Click.*

Oh, please.

I move the warm herbal pack to my knee, which is still very sore from the crash. There's just not that much room inside a crashing car. I mean, one's body tends to hit some very hard places.

"Oh, hey, it's Dr. D. again. I guess old Mrs. Sawyer called about getting some sleeping meds for her insomnia…hmm…she better come see me about it. Oh—unless she's too tired to drive. Well, hmm… Maybe you could arrange some transport for her? Or—I don't know—is it possible you could pick her up?…"

(*In spite of my aching body, I can feel my fists clenching.*)

"…I don't think she lives too far from—oh, wait a minute—I think you said your car was totaled. So, I wonder how you are getting in to work…hmm-m-m…Oh, hey—how are you, anyway? Better? Yeah, well, see what you can do to get Mrs. Sawyer in, OK? Good." *Click.*

…trying to find the joy…

Ben and I have lunch together, consisting of peanut butter

crackers and water. Better than nothing. He tells me he has his first guitar lesson scheduled and he's scared to death to take on the challenge. This is a side of him I've never seen before. He's always so laid-back and confident. His slightly disheveled grayish eyebrows have that crooked worry line. He looks so serious and sweet, almost boyish. Makes me want to cuddle him. I tell him:

"If you can call a few peanut butter crackers your lunch, then you can do anything."

{CHAPTER 29}

In which Katrinka climbs up and down the hills of her daily life
and finds a sweet surprise.

STOVE CITY
Dear Margery Casawill:
Are you aware that your extended service contract
on your Stove City microwave oven has expired?
Renew today!
Special rates...

To: FrRob@StPeter.org

From: Tink@maine.com

Fr. Rob,

After your mother died, did you get lots of junk in the mail for her?

Tink

To: Tink@maine.com

From: FrRob@StPeter.org

Tink,

Yup. I finally took one place up on their offer of a new charge account and 25% off coupon. I still remember the clerk's face at Flimsy Female Frocks when I showed up in my cassock. ☺

Fondly,

Fr. Rob

Ring. Ring. Beep. "It's Tink. And Ben. Leave a message."

"Tink? It's your brother, Richard. Hope your neck's feeling better. By the way, did I read somewhere that you are doing an advice blog? Cool. I'll have to check it out. Anyway—I'll come up Saturday to help clean out the storage units. Maybe I'll stay over. Hey, Ben— maybe we can do a short hike before I head back? Talk to you soon." *Click.*

Oh, boy. This is getting complicated. I pick up the phone to make a call. It rings and goes to voicemail.

Ring. Ring. Ring. Ring. Ring. Beep. "You've reached Dylan. What's up?"

"Dylan? It's Mom. Which weekend is it you guys are coming?"

Ring. Ring. Beep. "It's Tink. And Ben. Leave a message."

"Tink? It's Lorraine. Just wondered—can you make sure the house is dusted and vacuumed? My allergies are terrible lately. You still have that nice cleaning girl, right? Oh—are you feeling back to your old self yet? Love you." *Click.*

OK. My "nice cleaning girl" now has a *real* job. And my house hasn't been cleaned well for months. Normally, Ben vacuums a random room here or there when time allows. Which is completely CRAZY! Dirt from other rooms just gets tracked into the clean ones. God. In the old days, I'd get out my tiny little blue vacuum and do the other rooms he couldn't get to, but now my doctor won't let me even do that. Which is just plain…a bonus.

> **To: Lorraine@artist.com**
> **From: Tink@maine.com**
>
> Lorraine—No cleaning girl. Can't do much

preparation for your visit due to my injuries. Ben's been pretty busy—can't promise anything.

    xox Tink

To: Tink@maine.com
From: Lorraine@artist.com

    Don't worry. When I get there, I'll do it—just show me where everything is—vac, duster, polish, rags, etc. Hey—do you keep any of that baking soda freshener stuff for the carpets? Oh—and should I bring my own towels and washcloths? Or should I use your stuff? Except—wait—what kind of detergent do you use in your washer? And, do you use dryer sheets? If so, what kind? Just let me know. —L.

Ask Aunt Tink
Personal Advice for Your Personal Problems!

post a question | review account | emails recieved 19

Dear Aunt Tink,
I've been sharing an apartment with my boyfriend for 5 years. He has no money and he doesn't work. He says he'll know when the right job comes along. I work 12 hours a day down at the Truck Stop. Don't get me wrong, it's a good job, lots of tips. So I'm just wondering how I can get him to ask me to marry him?
—Waiting in Walla Walla

Oh, my God. I have no clue what to tell this woman that won't sound really lame. Or condescending. Or…

Dear Waiting,

Oo-o-o-o…tough problem. I probably can't give you (He is) any advice that you wouldn't already (a lazy, entitled) have heard from (jerk) your friends or family, so I'm not sure (you should kick) what (his sorry ass out) to tell you. (NOW!) But take a deep breath, relax, and maybe you will figure out…

(God Almighty. What is wrong with these people?!?)

…this difficult "puzzle" in your life.

Good luck!

Fondly,

Aunt Tink

Hope that'll go over OK. Hey—maybe people will stop writing to me. I mean, I don't mind the occasional call from a niece or nephew, but I don't have the time, or wisdom, to do more. What was Little Tink thinking? I'm sure she didn't intend to give me a chore. Come to think of it, she probably started this thing after a triple latte, feeling *really* upbeat. I've done things like that a lot. I've acquired best friends and new religions within minutes of a good cup of coffee. Little Tink—she's like my young twin sometimes. So fun-loving, so…oh, no. Another problem:

Dear Aunt Tink—

I'm beginning to think there really are differences between men and women. My boyfriend always has to prove things and fix stuff. How can I show him I'm always right about, well, everything?

—Marcie

Marcie,
You are always right! But guys like to think they are.

Great. That's not much of an answer. Hmm...

Marcie, here's an example of the gender difference: My fiancé Ben recently showed me an article about a woman named Josephine Baker who, at age 19, showed up in Paris in the 1920s and became a well-known and well-paid performer throughout Europe.
Here is the actual conversation we had about her:

Me: Wow! What'd she do? Sing? Dance?
He: She took off her clothes and paraded around the stage.

Marcie, he read that article with the same fervor he has while reading the latest medical research.

TODAY'S TIP: Whether you read professional journals, newspapers, or just fun books, get a little quiet time every day, people!

Ring. Ring. Beep. "(sigh) Tink. Message."
"Hi, Mom! It's Dylan! What's up? Mom, are you feeling any better? I hope so. Oh, about the weekend—well, it's not this weekend, it's the next. I'm pretty sure. Or the one after. I'll check with our ride."
Oh, Lord.
"And it's just gonna be me and Megan. Hope you're not disappointed Dan and his cousin can't make it."
Thank you, God.
"Love you!" *Click.*

Ring. Ring. Beep. "(Sigh). Tink. Message."

"Hi, Aunt Tink! It's Little Tink. I just wanted to tell you—you'll be totally excited—I posted on your blog that you are *fond of old-fashioned letter writing*!! You know, how you always send us stationery and stuff for birthdays? And it's such fun to get real letters. So much more personal. Oh, my God, I think *I* may actually turn into an 'Aunt Tink' someday. Wouldn't that be awesome? We're so much alike. I love letters, too. And coffee! Oh, and remember the great hikes and outings we had when I was younger and you packed all those snacks we both liked…"

And I remember the time we hiked up a small mountain after she had her first heartbreak. What was she, like 12? So bittersweet. Both of us crying together at one point, cursing men and eating through our sobs and shouts.

cute tissues for Little T/others for b-days & holidays etc.

"…I miss you, Aunt T. Well, anyway…if you get letters from people from your blog site, that's why. You probably won't get too many. I mean, who takes the time to write real letters anymore? Tell you what. I'll write you one. I love you. Mmmmwahhh!" *Click.*

Wow. Real letters? I love getting letters!
That sounds very, um, healing.

Our hero becomes the bearer of more burdens. We are privy to her innermost reflections.

You know those lower back muscles? And those muscles near the hip insertions? You know how you can only cold pack and hot pack a few areas at a time?

I think my "healing" (I am so tired of hearing that fucking term) is going to take a while.

Ring. Ring. Beep. "It's Tink. *Yes?*"

"Tink? Yeah, hi. It's Richard. Hey—Lorraine told me you were picking up some groceries for her for the weekend. So, she's coming up? I just wondered—if it's not too much, can you buy the stuff to make that chocolate cookie/whipped cream refrigerator cake for when I come up? I mean, can you actually make it, too? Mm-m-m... it would be so good! Just like, uh, you know...(sniff) argh, ah, just like when Mom was (sniff) alive. Oh, what would I do without you?"

And before the click, I hear his abbreviated choking sob.

I have *got* to find him a woman. I head out to the grocery store for everyone's requests.

And when I get home, I start making the refrigerator cake. I can't help but taste a little of the cake I'm making, the crisp chocolate wafer cookies with a little real whipped cream on them...When I see a broken-off piece, that's my sign that eating a little tonight was just meant to be. By tomorrow morning, after the whole cake sits in the fridge overnight, the wafers will soften next to the whipped cream, making black-and-white layers of yumminess. I'll have to caution Richard not to overdo it. He'd eat the whole cake by himself, given the chance.

~ ~ ~ ~ ~ ~ ~ ~

I occasionally make the mistake of calling my work voicemail from the kitchen phone at night, while I check the fridge to see if there's lunch food, just to get a jump on the next day. Sometimes I happen to find a stray piece of chocolate. I'm usually angry at myself for doing it. For checking messages, not having chocolate.

"Tink? Gloria. Hey, I'll need you to do the Injection Clinic this week. The regular Injection nurse had to go out of town, and there's really no one else to do it now. Hope this isn't a problem with your medical appointments. By the way, how's your neck and back? Hey, I didn't realize you have to wear a collar. Anyway—thanks. Really appreciate it." *Click.*

Shit.

I go upstairs to get ready for bed, and the answering machine light is flashing:

"Tink? Gloria."

Again!

"Hate to call you at home. But I just found out the geriatric team nurse was rushed to the hospital. Appendicitis. They wouldn't let her wait a week 'til what's-her-name gets back from wherever she went off to…"

Talk about your fount of compassion…

"…out for a couple of weeks. Afraid that leaves a bigger load of work for you and whoever's left. Maybe you could do some split shifts around your medical appointments? Thanks a million. Hey—I'm flying outta here—gotta go pick up the kids and head to my mother's up north. God, I hate that long drive. At least she's on the lake. Anyway, don't forget—I'm on vacation for the next week and a half. I had to forward my voicemail to your extension, but hopefully you won't get too many calls. Thanks! And hey—hope you're feeling better." *Click.*

I'm not, Gloria, thank you very much.

And on top of everything else, I have Mittelschmerz.

Look it up.

Do I have to teach you everything?!?

Damn.

{CHAPTER 31}

Our well-intentioned and increasingly agitated hero makes her
way through weekend events. We may wonder just how she will
fare, what with anticipated houseguests and yes, even weekend work
intrusion, a phenomenon not unheard of, lately, in the kingdom.
Keep in mind, Katrinka is attempting what is called,
in the vernacular of the day, self-soothing techniques.

I'm heading out the door for work when I hear my phone ringing.
And I keep going. Seeking peace? Walk past a ringing phone.

I have just enough time to get to Starbucks. My cell phone
goes off, but by the time I fish it out of my bag, it's stopped. No message,
but I see it's my cousin who called. It's several minutes before I get to
the next red light and can call my home phone number to retrieve any
messages.

"Hi, Tink. It's Lorraine. I think I'm just a few minutes away.
Can't find the directions. But I found a grocery store and picked up
those items I asked you to get. You probably didn't have time to go to
the store. Oo-o—hope you remembered to leave the door unlocked
for me. Oh, wait! I think I'm almost at your house. Looks familiar. See
you after work!"

Shit shit shit sh—

I go through the drive-up. Fortified enough by an iced café
mocha to face anything, I drive the few miles back home to unlock the
damn door. And give her a quick hug at the front door, where she is
trying to break in. ("I didn't want to call and bother you again!")

{*Chapter 31*}

Even though I am absolutely positive she has a copy of our house key. Like the directions, she can't seem to find it at first. But her retroactive retrieval system is remarkable. She's like a freaking St. Anthony, the way she finds lost things.

It hits me as I walk into work: the weekly morning meeting. I forgot again, and now I have to walk in late and feel like a big loser. I'm feeling sweaty from rushing around and having not a bad, but a terrible, hair day. It's going every which way but normal. I hate that. Ben loves it. Go figure.

As I enter the room, I hear Dr. Myers say, "…the Annual Nursing Competition."

All eyes are on me, and I get that "You're late!" look from the boss as I try to maneuver into a spare place to sit in this tiny room filled with dozens of people, all looking smug and feigning interest and stuff. At least Myers could've thanked me for volunteering to do the paper. Jeez.

Ben opens his eyes (God, I can't believe he's actually been napping not ten feet away from Dr. Myers in the staff meeting), and now he catches my eye and looks like he's trying very hard not to laugh at me. He subtly imitates playing a guitar and mouths "tonight." Huh? Oh! Tonight's his first lesson. Thought he was making some obscene gesture at me. I nod my head. Then I realize that nod has just signed me up for some new committee and now Dr. Myers is thanking me for volunteering. Shit shit shit.

Later, I periodically call home to listen to my home answering machine for some messages I'm expecting.

"Hi, Tink? This is Betsy from Physical Therapy Associates down in York…"

Oh, good. Finally.

"We origin-ly ha– you scheduled for Mon., Wed., and Fri. nex– week at one p– for your PT ap–nt, but –ks like we may ha– to mix

—at up a little. One of the therap—ts is ou— sick and pro—ly won't — back unti— at leas— mi—week. So when —ou get this, can you ca— me ri— away? I think you have —mber our —fice: —55-63—Oo-o-o. —ad connec—. Darned stati. Anyway, call me. Again the num— 4—crsp—jek— 2———grz—. Tha—ks!

I listen to it over and over and over and it sounds the same every single time.

After work, I stop to pick up some good take-out stuff from the big new (read "expensive") health food store. But it's worth it not to have to cook a meal that people will drift in and out of. Plus, they have the greatest marinated artichoke-heart salad. A pound of that and a few other things for protein, a featured cheddar from France—yum— some good bread…I nearly drop my teeth when the bill totals over $80 for one meal's worth.

I get home to find more than a dozen "fan" letters from blog readers. Unreal. Well, it's kind of interesting, as long as I don't have to write back. I bring in the letters with the groceries.

I know I'm not being a very gracious hostess and I'm not proud of it. But a crazy person has hidden me away somewhere and taken over my soul. When I get home, Lorraine is completely preoccupied with her beauty treatments, her laptop, and calling her daughter on the phone every hour to make sure she's having fun at her best friend's house. That part I get—the calling. But I just can't understand how she gets her nails—all 20 of them—so perfect and still manages to tap away at her computer constantly. She has unfortunately forgotten to put away the organic ice cream she got this morning at the grocery store. And somehow does not notice it dripping onto the kitchen counter, running over the scratched-up wooden drawers and metal handles, and into a little stream onto the floor.

I ignore the fact that she just doesn't see it. And also that she doesn't see me mopping it up, in all my soreness. I know she's a little spacey—an artist, after all. I'm trying to be loving and giving. But still. Dripping ice cream?

It is possible that I may have reacted with a little edginess. I'm not good at direct confrontation. Slamming drawers loudly is more my thing.

To: RichardC@NHschool.org
From: Lorraine@artist.com

Richard—hi. I'm here—in Maine. Boy, is Tink stressed-out! She got really, well, *bitchy* because I brought in groceries. How did I know she had gone to the store, too? Just trying to help. Now she's walking around muttering something about chocolate refrigerator cake and special muscle relaxation exercises. Big deal. I mean, I like to relax as much as the next guy. Maybe she should think about cutting back on the cake instead. Then she wouldn't have to do so much exercising. Anyway, you're coming over later, right? You and I should go to the storage units at some point and look over some stuff. Oh—wait. Tink has a big bag of supper stuff from Health Heaven! Good. I'm starving. See you later.

Lorraine

I walk upstairs to get some aspirin, and see my answering machine blinking.

"Hi, Tink! Betsy calling back from Physical Therapy Associates. Sorry about the phone connection earlier. Anyway—really need to hear back from you. Let's have y—come in t— our Scarb—— -fice t—— at two, OK? Call if y— Oh, damn! This stu— ph— ag— —n!! See y— then. Our numb— is 4–2—6——." *Click.*

I feel a slow burn rising, then I remember…*inner peace…God is here…inner peace…*

I hate to admit that some of the hackneyed phrases of the day they're promoting at work actually do help. Damn that stupid "mindfulness."

Ben doesn't get home until almost 9:00. But he looks like he really enjoyed his lesson. He's humming. Literally. He also smells like—well, he kind of has the aroma we all came to know and love back in the '60s, but I'm probably hallucinating from emotions at this point. Or from the marinated artichoke hearts, of which I ate fully half a pound myself.

My brother arrives and he and Ben have their heads together for the longest time over a couple of beers and some guy snacks, letting out huge bouts of laughter now and then. Before bed, Ben tells me they're getting up early for a jog around a nearby lake. Fine. I'm just the slave girl.

On Saturday, when I go to get the mail, I find this:

~ U.S.A. ~ POSTAL SERVICE ~ U.S.A. ~ POSTAL SERVICE ~

To: Katrinka Casawill, Water Street

Dear Katrinka Casawill:

Please see checked box below indicating a problem your mail carrier is having with your mail delivery. Please contact us at your earliest convenience to work with us in resolving the issue indicated below:

```
_ snow must be removed from mailbox area
  _ mailbox is damaged or otherwise unavailable
  _ mailbox quality has deteriorated and mail
delivery will be delayed until replacement is in
place
  X amount of mail delivered exceeds ability of
mailbox to contain mail
  Other:
```

Hi! Overload of mail began a few days ago. Please install larger box or make arrangements to pick up your mail at the Post Office. Thanks.
— Harry
P.S.—Will you be getting Martin and Marge Casawill's mail regularly? Just want to know. Probably should write it on your mailbox in case there's a substitute sometime.

My cousin and brother both stay for the weekend, during which time they look through exactly two large and one small box from the storage units, leaving more stuff scattered about and bringing back four more large boxes of junk to my home for me to look through because they think I'll enjoy the memories. Uh, maybe later, all right? For now, let me savor the far-off memory of my mother and father doing THEIR OWN business matters and my home looking like a home, not an extension of their storage units. Or a guest house. With a kitchen littered with dirty dishes and empty food containers, including the remnants of old, dried-out chicken salad. It is not a good smell.

What's with me? I used to be so easygoing. I guess my mom's death and my screwed-up hormones are taking their toll. Not to mention near-constant pain. But other than that…

At the end of the weekend, Richard takes the bulk of the refrigerator cake with him, hugging me and outright weeping, and my cousin asks me if I want her to wash the linens she used. She tells me it was "the best visit ever!" and promises "I'll call you."

Oh.

Well...gosh.

I call Adeline and we chat on the phone, the way we did in person before all this chaos began. We make a promise to get together for a spontaneous walk or cup of tea.

I've got a couple of hours to rest before bed. Tomorrow is, after all, Monday.

My beeper goes off.

It's the hospital.

Ext. 2005?

Voice: Emergency Room Registration, may I help you?

Me: Yeah...this is Tink Casawill. I'm a nurse in the Outpatient Clinic. Well, I'm home right now—but did someone there page me?

Voice: Oh!! *Yes!* Thanks for calling back. We have a Mrs. Johnson who isn't feeling well and has been seen in the ER. It looks like we'll be keeping her overnight. Probably just a bit of flu. Do you know what kind of insurance she has? She's a little confused, but she says she's Dr. D.'s patient.

Me: Dr. D.'s patient?

Voice: Yes. Anyway, we really need to know what she has for insur—

Me: And you paged me because...?

Voice: Well, we tried Dr. D. first.

Me: He probably wouldn't know.

Voice: Well, uh, his voicemail says to page you.

Me: Look, I'm really sorry to hear the patient is ill, but I HAVE NO IDEA ABOUT HER #^%#*%&*%^*$ INSURANCE, AND WHEN I GET MY HANDS ON DR. D. HE'D BETTER HAVE SOME INSURANCE OF HIS OWN!!!!!!!

~ ~ ~ ~ ~ ~ ~ ~

Sunday evening, I walk down the long driveway to our mailbox and tape a handwritten label to our mailbox that lists my parents' names under Ben's, Dylan's, and my name. A little earlier, Ben went over to the big-box hardware store and now we have a second mailbox. It looks like a fucking commune lives here.

Harry—
Can you sell me a couple of rolls of 100 first-class stamps?
—Tink
P.S.—Let me know amount—I'll leave a check. Thanks!
And—yeah, I'll probably be getting Marge and Martin's
mail for a while.

Thank God I have a very helpful and kind postman.

Incr. Harry's Xmas bonus—? hide out in
mail truck when fam. here—read fan mail
someday—

Katrinka faces preparation for battle—all in the day of a true hero with a heart of gold and a mouth like a sailor.

This is a long one. I recommend it be accompanied by tea and possibly something nutritious in the slightly sweet category. Half a piece of apple pie works well. OK, a whole piece. Just let's move on now.

Monday morning.

I'm at work, I have my Starbucks, and I'm optimistic. Feeling relaxed. Princess-ish. Remembered to put on my delicious Crabtree and Evelyn body lotion.

But…uh…Remember that children's book about the awful, lousy, no-good, etc., day? Well, here's the *adult* version. And, sadly, I do not mean that in a sexy way.

First thing, I check my messages, forwarding a few. I jot down names and numbers that are non-urgent call-backs. I do this while I'm writing up the outline for the nursing paper.

"Tink? It's Phys– Therap– –sociates. Hope it's –K to phone y– at w–k. W– really need to he– fr– you –out the –pointment. You have — number. Thanks!" *Click.*

and then:

"Hi, Tink, this is Jonathan R. Remember me? I guess I'm supposed to use the refill line, but Dr. D. specifically told me to tell *you…*"

What if I just forward this to Dr. D.?

Oh, yeah. It would come right back to me.

~ ~ ~ ~ ~ ~ ~ ~

I go to the staff room to fax some insurance forms. The staff room, on a good day, is total chaos, with over 40 staff members on our floor alone, in and out constantly. It gets pretty crowded at times. Years ago, there was a rumor that someone got pregnant at work. Accidentally. I'm pretty sure it happened between the fax machine and the recycle bin. I really do think it was accidental.

Back at my desk, I have a whole batch of new voicemails.

"Nurse Tink? It's Emily, Dr. Green's patient? Gotta be quick— don't have many minutes left on this cell phone. That refill line keeps cutting me off. Can you call my meds in to the hospital pharmacy? Except the tranquilizer. Can you call that one in to my regular place? The super-pharmacy over in that new health food store? Really cheap…"

Sure it is. But then they get you on the fabulous artichoke hearts and French cheese…

"…Oh, and I wonder if they have any good deals on vitamins? Because I think I might be—oops! Gotta go. Boyfriend's here!!!" *Click.*

Then Dr. Jane buzzes me and asks me to do something that amounts to a wild goose chase. Looking up old records (if we even have them), numerous phone calls, all because of various parts of our "electronically mission-driven system of health care," to quote Dr. Boring—I mean, Dr. Myers.

For Dr. Jane, I'd do anything. She's such a treat. We clicked the moment she arrived here a few years ago. We get each other's humor, we share problems, and both love dark chocolate. That's a bond not to be taken lightly. And she's her own person, as a doc. I'm happy to help her, and she never dumps her own work on me. Sometimes I have to insist she let me do more. Ugh. She should be Queen.

Concerned about "Emily," I leave a message for Dr. Green, looking for a current phone number for this patient.

No sooner do I hang up but my voicemail light is blinking again.

"Yeah, hi, Tink. Dr. D. here. Calling from the conference..."

Oh, yeah, I forgot. He's at the Excellence (ha-ha) in Medical Practice seminar today.

"...Yeah—hey, I called in a prescription for Mrs. Stewartson Friday after I saw her, and it turns out she'll need a prior authorization before her insurance company will pay for it. Can you take care of that? I think the rationale should be in the computer, dictated from Friday afternoon. Thanks very much." *Click.*

OK, fine. Whatever.

> **To: KatrinkaC@MeHosp.org**
> **From: Medical Records@MeHosp.org**
>
> Gee, Tink, I don't know how long it takes for the dictations to get into the computer system. Couple of business days, I think. Hope that helps! Hey, how are you feeling?
>
> Nina

Voicemail light is blinking again. Dr. Green has no number for Emily.

"What's your concern?"

Two minutes later:

"So, yeah, Tink. Dr. D. again. You know, I was thinking…the dictation on Mrs. Stewartson probably isn't up yet…"

No kidding, Kreskin.

"Uhh…let's see…depression, hasn't responded to other meds… how's that?"

Isn't he supposed to be at a seminar?

Can he not just sit in his seat and listen to the lecturer and stop calling me?

> **To: KatrinkaC@MeHosp.org**
> **From: MyersE@MeHosp.org**
>
> Tink, I got a message on my voicemail this morning from the supervisor in ER Registration. It sounds like you had a meltdown or something. What's going on? Are you feeling stressed in some way? If so—hey—I'm here to help!

~ ~ ~ ~ ~ ~ ~ ~

Two hours, 21 phone calls, eight insurance Prior Authorizations, and no lunch later, I pick up my purse to go across the street to pick up a quick sandwi—

Ring. Ring. Sigh. Caller ID can be such a curse if you have a conscience.

"Yes?"

"It's Dr. D. All I can say is 'Oops!' Really sorry—but can you re-do the prior authorization on Mrs. Stewartson? She does have depression, but she also has *high blood pressure*. Hang on. (sneeze) Uh-oh…cold coming on. Better get more lozenges…Anyway, Tink, about Mrs. Stewartson—that's why we need to try a different antidepressant than the one on the insurance company's formulary. Don't want her to have a stroke or anything…"

You big dope.

I wait. I know there's more. And I'll bet he's missing the crux of the seminar—like the part that talks about actually having eye contact with patients. Or about not having a meltdown any time he actually needs to help someone and not just write out a prescription.

"So I put her on…uh…agh, darn it! I guess—can you check RX Compu-Plus on the computer and see what I discontinued and what I put her on? Before 2:00?"

It's 1:59.

I gently hang up. Don't want to cause a scene. Don't want to look "stressed."

Fuck. Putting lunch on hold, I run—well, limp—between the phone and the staff room looking for the necessary form to do all this.

2:10 p.m.

"Tink? This is Amy at WeCareRX. Yes, you're
correct. Requests need to be faxed to us no later
than two p.m. to ensure an answer by five p.m. But
get it to us by three o'clock, mark it 'Urgent,'
and we should have an answer for you by six."

You know, Amy sounds nice. Wonder if Richard…ugh! I've got to stop this. The last match I tried to make for him, a while back, was a total disaster. I'd arranged for them to meet at a holiday sing-along. Music is Richard's life, and she'd seemed really interested in meeting him. Turns out she sang completely off-key and apparently quite loudly, and oh, yeah, she was completely smashed. He'd called me to ask where to "deliver" her.

To: KatrinkaC@MeHosp.org
From: Help Desk@RXPlus.com

* AUTO-REPLY * PLEASE DO NOT RESPOND TO THIS E-MAIL *

We have received your e-mail. The program "RXCompu-Plus" is temporarily down. We are working on it and should have it repaired by tomorrow morning. Thank you for your inquiry.

Deep breath. I begin the trek to and through Medical Records to find the information I need.

Lorraine calls.

"I'm calling you at your work number, right? Well, anyway, I think I may have left a sketchpad I was working on at your house and it's pretty important. I'm preparing a portfolio to present in less than a week. Can you look around at home and call me? Love you!" *Click.*

And, then, like finding a long-lost missing puzzle piece behind a scary, hairy, fuzz-clumped sofa cushion:

"Nurse Tink? It's Emily. (sniff) I called the pharmacy and they said you didn't call in my meds and they're closing soon. I'm still at my (sniff) boyfriend's. His number is (sniff) 555-0164." *Click.*

So I call 555-0164 and get a message that starts off with Guns and Roses' "Welcome to the Jungle" for a full minute, followed by "Hey—It's Nick. Leave a fuckin' message, dude."

To which I answer: "Yeah, dude, this is Nurse Tink, at your girlfriend's fuckin' doctor's office. Hey—I need to talk to Emily before I can call in her prescriptions. And, like, I'm fuckin' outta here, like, real soon, man. So have her call me."

I leave him with a few bars of "Spoonful of Sugar" from *Mary Poppins*.

Buzz. Buzz. I grab the phone.

"Hello? Oh, Emily! I'm really glad you called back…Yes, I know adults don't usually talk like that…Uh-huh…uh-huh…well, thank you, Emily. I'm glad you think I'm cool for an older lady. Huh? Oh, um, sure, I'd love to come hear your man's band sometime. Um, Emily, I just wanted to know why you were so interested in getting vitamins. Uh-huh…uh-huh…oh. Oh!!! Yes, yes! I think it indeed may help you ward off *that little cold*. Huh? Oh, yes. Yes. I'll call your meds right in."

And of course, by the time I get off the phone, the hospital pharmacy is closed, I have to call back and leave a fuckin' message on her boyfriend's fuckin' voicemail, and OK, I offer to help pay the extra couple of bucks for her to pick them *all* up at her regular pharmacy, which cheerfully accepts my credit card.

6:15 p.m. I call home to check our home phone's voice messages. Why don't I just have the phone surgically implanted into my brain already?!?

"Tink—It's me, Ben. Your Loved One. Hey—It's 5:30 and I'm still at the office. Wondered if you wanted to meet me downtown for supper. Japanese? I'll be leaving the office in a bit. I figure you're probably home resting or eating chocolates in front of the TV, right? Ha-ha, just kidding. So call me back. I love you."

HE LOVES ME *AND* HE WANTS TO GO OUT FOR JAPANESE FOOD!?! YAY!!!!!!!!!!!!!!

I call Ben back and get his voicemail. I suppose I could just walk down the hallway and up the two flights of stairs to get to his office. But the headphone set is already on my head, and I'm tired and achy.

And he's probably in the middle of dictating notes anyway.

"Ben—It's me. Just called home and picked up the message you left me about supper. Are you still here? I haven't left yet either. I'm swamped. Probably can get out of here in maybe a half hour. Still want to eat out? I am *really* hungry and having a lot of pain."

get out of f-ing work earlier EVERY DAY!!!!!! fig. out why doing too much shit all time—

A little while later, I try again.

"Ben—are you still there? Ben? Ben? Be—?"

Oh, damn.

7:10 p.m.

Buzz. Buzz. Beep. "You've reached the voicemail for Katrinka Casawill at the Outpatient Clinic. Please leave a detailed message and I will return your call. For the Prescription Refill line, press four. For emergencies, press zero."

"Sweetie? It's Adeline. Sorry to call you at work, but something tells me you might still be there. Are you OK? Please take care of yourself. Call me. Maybe we can get together soon? Like we talked about."

Oh…I remember those fun days. Looks like I'll have to actually schedule something, like an appointment, and not rely on spontaneity.

8:30 p.m.

I am just getting my coat on to leave the office when my phone starts ringing again.

{Chapter 32}

Buzz. Buzz. Bee—

Oh, crap. I am NOT going to pick up. I'm NOT. I'm NOT. I'm…I'm…

I understand the concept of voicemail and walking away, but I FORGET, OK? I'm 54. Perimenoshit. Sometimes I can ignore the phone or a waiting voicemail. But I am still thinking Ben and miso soup, that he might still be in the building and ready to sweep me off my feet in the direction of a steaming dish of salmon teriyaki and all the yumminess that goes with it. I turn to pick it up. Too late. Already gone to voicemail.

I can't let it go. I listen.

"Hello? Hello? Oh. Well, maybe you've gone home, Nurse Tink. This is Mrs. Stewartson calling…"

Aaarrrggghhhhh!

"…I'm a patient of Dr. D. I'm calling about getting my prescription approved. My antidepressant. It's *very important.* I'm calling to see if it's gone through yet. Can you call me back, dear? My pharmacy closes in a half an hour. Thank you! Oh—I'm at my sister's on her, uh, cellular phone. Let me see what the number is. Oh, wait. Liz? Liz? Do you know what the—oh, wait, dear. Maybe if I push this button—"

Uh-huh. The sounds of silence.

I am constitutionally unable to leave something for a patient undone. So I call the hospital operator, tell her it's an emergency, she gets a special dispensation from the Pope, and traces the number, something that works only for certain numbers, apparently. I call Mrs. Stewartson and tell her I'm working on it and will call her the minute I have an answer.

Act of Kindness accomplished.

Japanese food unattainable.

{CHAPTER 33}

Katrinka, malnourished and fatigued, discovers her expanded repertoire of multitasking.

I get home from work at 9:00 and am overcome with the comforting delicious smell of KFC. Ben is watching *Law and Order*. I hear the final chords of justice emanating from the TV, just as he finishes the last slurping bite from a bucket of chicken. "Original" style, my favorite, nothing but a pile of bones left. Damn. Damn. Damn.

The dog looks curiously satisfied.

I put my things down on the ever-growing mountain of junk on the kitchen table. I quickly sort through the heap of papers and fan mail, looking for Lorraine's sketchpad. Nothing. But then I spot more mail for my departed mom:

******** **MARGE CASAWILL** ********
IT'S NEVER TOO LATE FOR FINE DINING!
WOODED PINE PARK'S
SENIOR LIVING, MEALS ARE SERVED WHEN *YOU* WANT THEM!

PLEASE JOIN US FOR A COMPLIMENTARY ROAST TURKEY DINNER...

Turkey? Gravy? I'm starving.

I kiss a sleepy-looking Ben and say nothing about the dinner-that-was. I just can't.

As I head upstairs, the phone rings. It's Ali. We talk as I head downstairs to the kitchen, passing Ben and the empty food containers.

"Hi, Mom! I'm just calling to talk about the summer and coming up to Maine for vacation. John and I thought maybe we could all go somewhere for a few days. Lake or ocean."

I could use a vacation right about now. Someplace where there's a lot of food.

"Oh, that would be fun," I say, "but let me call you back, honey, 'cause I just got in a few minutes ago and I HAVEN'T EATEN YET. *HAVE I, BEN !?!?!* THAT IS, ONE OF US HAS NOT EATEN YET."

The TV is now blaring the opening music theme (da-dum dum dum dum dum dummmmm) of the next episode of *Law and Order*.

Ben: Zzzzzzzzzzzzzzzzzzzz…

"Ali? He isn't even listening. I'll call you later after I get some food."

I wish I could stop thinking about chocolate mousse mocha cake. And the chicken. How could he? When I think of all the times I make dinner for him, and yes, You Take the Bigger Plate…Oh No Sweetie—Really —It's Fine You Take It…

I settle for low-fat fake cheese product (a poor substitute for American cheese, at least it's organic; I'll pretend to like it) on whole wheat with tomatoes. Certainly not KFC. I try to give the dog a piece of cheese product, and he actually snubs it.

I wake up sometime later on the love seat, my Skinny-Frozen-Pretend-Gourmet ice cream dish nearby, empty, spoon hanging off of it, and a note on top.

Sweetheart—
I'm sorry. I must have dozed off watching TV.
Wish we hadn't missed each other earlier. I had no
idea you were still stuck at the clinic, poor baby.
I love you bunches. Oh—there's a card for you on
the kitchen table—looks like it's from Fr. Rob.
Ben

I go to the table and look through what seems to be the newer mail, looking for the card.

Oh. My. God.
Where did all these bills come from, postmarked weeks ago?!?!?!

And what's this postcard for Ben with a handwritten smiley face on it? I normally wouldn't look at his mail. But it's just a postcard. Everyone knows it's OK to read postcards. That's the rule. Even the mailman can read them, including Harry, who a while back told me my Pap was negative as he handed me the mail at the base of our driveway.

I turn over the postcard. Oh. A reminder card for his next guitar lesson. But…smiley face? Oh! Oh, that's so cute! The studio must have a lot of young students. I look back at the growing chaos on the table.

It is possible I would have more patience with all this if it weren't for the fact that I'm trying to DECREASE MY CAFFEINE per Dr. Know-It-All's orders. Well, we'll just see what good it does for my breasts. I can pretty well predict it won't do as much as a trip to Victoria's Secret.

Ha. Smiley face. Cute.

~ ~ ~ ~ ~ ~ ~ ~

I am not deceived. That call from Ali about vacation plans was just the beginning of a series of no less than 50 phone calls and e-mails that will throw both of us into the worst state of confusion since the Treaty of Versailles.

Since I'm the one living in Maine, the vacation destination, I check with friends, coworkers, and relatives, all of whom have differing recommendations and opinions. I end up calling the "Chamber of Worthless Pamphlets" agencies in five different coastal towns, none of which will recommend anything other than to check the listings on their website, and they seldom list prices. Why do they even have employees at these places? They must have to take an oath to never, ever recommend a place. They don't budge. I've even tried bribery. If the government ever wants a truly tight security system, they should hire these people.

I have just about enough energy left to crawl to the sink to brush my teeth and get ready for—

Ring. Ring. Beep. "It's Tink. Your message?"

"Tink? Tink?!? It's Dad! I need to talk to you. Can you—"

I pick up. I'm tired, but I love my Dad and even with frequent visits, he—and I—find our contact very comforting. There's a sweetness that has developed more in our relationship since my mom died.

"Hi, Dad. How are you?" I ask, and discover I can actually sit on the computer chair, talk with my father on speaker phone, brush my teeth, do my gentle stretching exercises Dr. Alfred gave me, and snooze a little, all at the same time.

All part of my taking-care-of-self routine.

get smiley face stckrs & others for gr-kids—

send p-cards more—? cards w/$1 in ea.—try

send. more oft.—? wkly?

{CHAPTER 34}

After many unpleasant experiences and subsequent utterances, Katrinka finds herself led to things more spiritual.

Tuesday work. Getting ready.

     Makeup, hair, putting on some—

     Putting on some—

Hold on.

Oh. My. God.

I have a, um, hair. Coming out of my…ear.

Not the positive change I was hoping to see in myself.

INSTANT REPLAY—PLEASE EXCUSE PREVIOUS
INTERRUPTION and thank you in advance for *NEVER
MENTIONING IT AGAIN.*

{CHAPTER 35}

After many unpleasant experiences and subsequent utterances, Katrinka finds herself led to things more spiritual.

Tuesday work. Getting ready. Better be better than Monday work. P.S.—It isn't.

I am on my way to the clinic. So far, a gas truck has cut me off, a teenaged driver in front of me has thrown a lit cigarette out the window, landing a little too close to my car for comfort (I hate it when I have to wonder if my gas tank's about to blow up. I'd like to lecture the little bugger in a major way) and another idiot has pulled out in front of me while laughing on her cell phone.

Is road rage really such a bad thing? Couldn't it be thought of as self-expression?

OK, it's true that these are all near-misses in the world of motor vehicle collisions.

But it does not feel good when my cherished iced café mocha spills all over me and the front seat.

In the work bathroom, I attempt to get out a rather interesting pattern of coffee stains from my pastel outfit using a technique I once read about, which actually makes it a lot worse. I end up using the old sweater-hanging-off-the-waistline method that was so useful back in junior high when one gets surprised by her monthly "friend."

I hate the feeling of damp pants.

{*Chapter 35*}

Check phone messages. Print out the list of upcoming in-services. Printer still doesn't work. But at least the office manager has put in a work order. That is a major accomplishment, even though it means absolutely nothing as to when or if the printer will someday work.

I take what I can.

All my phone lines are going at once, but I listen to some of my messages first.

"Tink? It's Dr. D. Not sure where we're at with Mrs. Stewartson and that Prior Authorization, but I picked up a call from her saying you didn't call her back. Well…uh, can you get right on that today, because, jeepers, she's going to Hawaii for a week. I guess she inherited a bunch of money from somewhere. She's taking a bunch of friends and her kids and grandkids with her. You know, gosh, it seems like maybe she could have just paid for the new medicine out of pocket. It's only like three bucks or so. Hmm…well, thanks for checking up on it." *Click.*

I pick up the phone. As I leave Dr. D. the following voicemail message, my printer, like the biblical miracle of the loaves and the fishes, begins popping out multiple copies of the in-service schedule. Fuck it. Lose a few trees. The irony of the work order finally being in place is not lost on me.

Like a pot of spaghetti boiling over, I leave this voicemail:

"Dr. D.? Tink here. Yeah. I'm taking care of Mrs. Stewartson and her meds. I STAYED HERE 'TIL EIGHT THIRTY FRIDAY NIGHT THANK YOU VERY MUCH AND I BELIEVE I TOLD YOU THAT I WOULD TAKE CARE OF IT, AS WELL AS THE CHANGES YOU LEFT ME IN ALL YOUR MESSAGES YESTERDAY WHILE YOU WERE AT THE CONFERENCE AND IF YOU EVER MENTION NICE MRS. STEWARTSON'S NAME AGAIN I WILL PERSONALLY DISMANTLE EVERY CHART IN

YOUR STACK AND SHRED YOUR SUPERBILLS!!!!!!!!!!!!!!!!!
Golly gee, have a good day, Doctor." *Click. Slam.*

Hmm. Maybe that was a bit impulsive. Hope they included a lecture on having a sense of humor at the seminar. Oh, well. Too late now. See? That's what happens to me sometimes when I get overwhelmed. Oh, and fuck you, perimenopause.

Yeah. Well, anyway.

I pull out a high-calorie but really yummy and possibly healthy granola bar. I'm lying. I pull out three. And eat them all with a cup of coffee from the staff room. I pass Nellie in the hallway and have a brief chat with her about this whole taking care of self/wellness junk.

Just to add to the beauty of this already doomed day, they start fixing the plumbing in the entire building, right in the middle of a busy clinic. All bathrooms are out of order. No water. They finally put up the "Out of Order" signs an hour after the repair work began. Which still does not stop people from using the bathrooms.

As I walk by the bathroom, I ask a staff member who is walking out if she needs some hand sanitizer and she says (I SWEAR TO GOD):

"Why?"

Yuck.

I'm back at my work desk, three phone lines ringing, and I'm on the fourth.

"You need to go to the ER," I tell my patient on the other end. "I mean, you're having trouble walking? And talking? Yes. Hold on. We'll get you some help. What? No, this cannot wait 'til tomorrow. That's right...yes...tell your son he'll have to get to tonight's game some other way. I know his activities are very important to him. Huh? I don't know if he'll be mad at you, but..."

To: Tink@maine.com

From: NellieR@MeHosp.org

Tink—

I've thought this over. No. Getting pregnant at 54 is *not* a good way to conceal midriff bulge.

Nellie

Buzz. Buzz. Beep. "You've reached the voicemail for Katrinka Casawill at the Outpatient Clinic. Please leave a detailed message and I will return your call. For the Prescription Refill line, press four. For emergencies, press zero."

"Hello, Katrinka? This is Betsy from Physical Therapy Associates. I got your work number from your PCP's office. You missed your appointment Friday afternoon. I'm not sure if I'll be able to schedule you here for another appointment without checking with my supervisor. Please call as soon as possible. I think you have our number." *Click.*

"Hello. This is Amy from WeCareRX. We have approved your request for the new medication for Mrs. Stewartson."

Finally. The end of the Mrs. Stewartson escapade.

"Can you tell her the co-pay will...let's see...tier three... that's twenty-f

Click.

Twenty-five dollars? *$25?!?* Dr. D. said that med only costs around $3 OUT-OF-POCKET!!!!

What's the equivalent of road rage on the phone?

"Tink? This is Hannah at your doctor's office. Uh, we got a call from Physical Therapy Associates saying that you have not been showing up for your PT appointments. Dr. Alfred is very concerned.

Yours is a serious condition and the treatment will make a huge difference in your recovery. Please call them to reschedule. I believe you have their number. If not, give us a call." *Click.*

Which I do. Because…oh, this is getting so tiring…I do not know which of the hundreds of physical therapy places in Southern Maine is the right one. It's mathematically amazing how the words "physical," "therapy," "greater," "Portland," "Southern," "Maine," and "associates" can be configured into over 200 forms. Well, close to that. I mean, doesn't anybody open any burger joints anymore?

I call back my PCP's office.

"Hello. You have reached the offices of Dr. Alfred and Dr. Kazelli. The office is closed for the day. We will reopen tomorrow. Please call back then. If this is an emergency, hang up and dial nine-one-one." *Click.*

OK, I'll just try to figure it out again from the phone book. While I'm at work *trying to do my job.*

Twelve more medication requests, three insurance forms, eight community referrals—all have fallen into my Inbox in the last ten minutes. The miracles just never stop.

Shit. Now I can't find my glass—

Oh. There they are.

Under my shoe.

I'll have to call the operator for the PT's number. And put it on my calling card. Well, one little Information call shouldn't use up too many minutes on the card. Cheaper than using minutes up on my cell phone.

Operator: Ma'am, there are fifty-four listings in your area that have the words "physical therapy associates" in their name. Would you like all of them?

Me: Um, OK.

Operator: Well, I can only give you one at a time. You'll have to call back for the others. Which one would you like?

~ ~ ~ ~ ~ ~ ~ ~

To: KatrinkaC@MeHosp.org
From: GloriaT@Sunnyhills.com

    Tink. You OK? The reason why I ask is that
Dr. D. called me—on my vacation, the jerk—said
you kind of fell down on an important task.
Doesn't really sound like you, you're such a
perfectionist. Anyway, can we meet next Monday to
talk about it? Oh—actually, I'm taking Monday off
for the holiday. You working? Yeah. I think you're
scheduled. Well, I'll see you next Tuesday, then.
Have a great week!

Hmm…how does getting lectured fit into my self-care plan?

~ ~ ~ ~ ~ ~ ~ ~

Later, at home, I stain-stick the hell out of the mocha stains on my clothes and get comfy.

To: Tink@maine.com
From: FrRob@StPeter.org

    Dear Tink,
    I'm sure God will forgive you ☺ for giving, um,
"the finger" ☹ to that other driver this morning.
Also to the visually impaired person who was in
the crosswalk. ☹ ☹ She probably couldn't see you

anyway. You were, after all, hurrying to get to work, with patients waiting for you and your warm gift of compassion. ☺

One Hail Mary ought to do it. ☺ ☺ ☺

And a nice cup of coffee. Hey, what's this about decreasing caffeine? I believe the Good Lord would want you to be happy. AND HAVE COFFEE.

Fr. Rob

P.S.—Yes, I think it is part of anyone's ministry to enjoy a "tall one" after work with one's loved one.

Isn't he great? Just like a priest ought to be. I'll have to remember him in my prayers tonight. After my stretches and packs and…yeah, prayers are definitely in order. And a little extra caff in my iced mocha tomorrow.

…peace…serenity now…peace…caffeine tomorrow…

{Chapter 36}

In which our hero reconnects with the younger and elder heirs to the throne whilst performing the usual assortment of royal duties.

The next few days pass in a slightly less hectic manner, which is good because I was getting close to the point of needing to really escape—like moving to a far-off hut in the woods somewhere. After work Friday, I pick up a voicemail from Dylan.

"Hi, Mom! It's Dylan. What's up? Yeah, I don't think we'll be there this weekend. Probably the next instead. Oh, yeah, and I'm bringing some of my winter stuff back with me that I won't need here at school. Just a few bagfuls of things to store. And some laundry to do. I figure I might as well save it up, you know? But don't worry. I'll do it. Love you!" *Click.*

OK, for those of you without college-aged kids, or who have blocked it out, it goes something like this: Beloved Child and Cherished Girlfriend arrive home, give warm hugs, and tolerate six minutes of polite conversation about school life, current activities, and general catching up. Beloved Child's cell phone rings. I know. Sometimes it happens before the six minutes are up. B.C. says into phone, "Hey, man, can I call you back?" Then B.C. brings several mountains of laundry from somewhere outside the house into the laundry room, and with lots of encouragement—OK, gentle pleading—puts the first load of laundry into the washer. Cell phone rings again.

"Hey, Mom. Craig is coming over. He's home from Spain. We're gonna go out for pizza, OK?"

A long series of washing, drying, and folding of clothes continues all weekend, by Indulgent Adoring Mommy (the great I AM). There are intermittent two- to three-minute episodes of chat, an occasional hug or two, and usually one family meal out, Chinese or Mexican. And a DVD at home, during which, and no longer than 46 minutes into said DVD, B.C. and C.G. go out with friends again, at 10 p.m. Then the weekend is over, and the B.C. is hauling eight large garbage bags full of clean, folded laundry into friend's car, with great and profuse "Thanks, Mom!'s" and a final few hugs before B.C. and C.G. head back to school and I AM has a good cry.

The only thing that stops the tears is going upstairs to B.C.'s room to view what can only be described as the aftermath of a natural disaster.

And guess what?

This is the scenario that actually begins just hours after picking up his message. At close to 10 p.m., I hear a car pull into the driveway, just as I'm heading toward the mail pile. Turns out it *is* the weekend Dylan and his girlfriend are coming to visit.

OK, then. My boy's here!! And that's a good thing.

Dylan's cell phone rings, and he wanders around the kitchen talking while I make small talk with his girlfriend. He hangs up.

"Mom? Megan and I are heading out to see Mike and Lisa downtown, OK? See you later. Don't worry—we won't be out too late."

I look at the clock: 10:30 p.m.

~ ~ ~ ~ ~ ~ ~ ~ ~

SHIT! THE BLOG. THE DAMNED BLOG.

Dear Aunt Tink,
I've been selling my body for several years now and have managed to earn quite a tidy living, even by New York standards. The trouble is my rent's going up and my customers are complaining that my prices—

Aaaarrrrgggghhhh!!!!

I can't even begin to help this poor girl. I mean, I know *nothing* about negotiating rent.

It's late. Time to rest. Time to spend a few precious moments with Ben, who is…? Sounds like he's talking on the phone. But at this hour? His portable phone is not in its cradle. Could be anywhere in this big house. But I guess I'm wrong, because he's just sitting at his computer, fiddling, when I find him. I give him a hug, then hear my phone going off.

Ring. Ring. Beep. "It's Tink. Your message?"

"Hi, Mom! It's Ali. I know it's kinda late, but I just got done making up the kids' lunches for the church field trip tomorrow and getting fruit cut up for breakfast…"

How is it that my daughter is so much younger than me but she's so much more organized? Am I what's called over the hill? Am I deteriorating?

"…Anyway—just wondered if you found out anything about places to stay on our fun vacation. Call me when you can. Love you!"

And then, just the kind of supportive message I need:

To: Tink@maine.com

From: FrRob@StPeter.org

Dear Tink,

To answer your recent question: I do believe that just because a person is not with us on earth, their spirit may indeed visit us. In my seminary training, however, I do not recall learning that a spirit could directly lead people to eat chocolate desserts against their will. But I do not rule anything out for true believers.

Always,

Fr. Rob

{Chapter 37}

It becomes clear that our hero must work very hard to arrange some well-deserved respite from her daily tasks.

Saturday morning. I know Dylan and his friend will be sleeping until at least 1 p.m. So I go about my day.

I am at my local auto travel office with the travel associate, formerly known as representative, formerly known as specialist, formerly known as agent (for *the love of…!*), and she basically opens travel books and looks online. Yeah. Just like I can. Why am I even here?

Me: (pointing to her computer screen) That hotel there? Is it clean?

Auto Girl: Clean? Um, probably.

What happened to the days when these people knew something?

Here I am in a renowned travel agency, and it feels like I'm in the middle of a big-box store, asking the twelve-year-old sales "whatever" if there are any navy blue pants in my size.

"Um…if we had any, they'd be out?" she'd say, with her snotty, sneering voice going up, as if to say *What are you, stupid? Like, we don't have any storage space out back anymore, ever.* Oh. So, things come off the truck and proceed nonstop onto the racks? Please.

Sorry. Moody moment. Damn GYN. I swear he put a curse on me.

Oh—vacation planning.

So, although it's Saturday, my day off, I've done my homework and I've already learned about more than 20 lovely coastal possibilities for the family vacation.

And that's OK, because in the midst of my inquiries, my daughter Ali in NC is also doing her part, ordering booklets and brochures and visiting her library to read about the Maine coast. And you know what? This *is* gonna be fun.

Back home, doing chores, Ben out in the garage, no sign of life from Dylan's room or the guest room.

Ring. Ring.

Ali: Mom, how do you feel about looking at some places more *inland*?

I hide the noose from myself. See, my friend Jill, a former travel agent, has suggested some place she knows about on the coast. And who knows if it's what Ali and John have been looking for, but on a whim, just as a backup, I've made reservations in case we don't find anything else we like better. But forget all that, because that's just our "safety school," if you know what I mean. Now Ali is talking about finding a place *away* from the coast. And please note, my friend Jill (see list of characters—OK, she's not there—just pencil her in) is NOT, I repeat, NOT afraid to speak up. Get that, Chamber (Worthless) Pamphlet Nazis!

Uh, where was I? Oh yeah—

Me (in my most loving Mom voice): Inland, sweetheart?

(My loving Mom voice is yet another attempt to repair any damage I might have done during her growing up years. She was my first, after all.)

Still Me: That would be OK, but what part of Maine?

She: Oh—north, I think. Katie! "North"—spell it, please— Or south, Mom. Good, Katie! Or the Lakes Region. Now "region," Katie—or—maybe the White Mountains in New Hampshire? Oh. Gotta go! We're late! *Shit.* No, Katie—please do *not* spell that word— ELLIOTT!!!!!!!!!!!!!!!!!!!! VIOLIN CLASS!!!!!!!!!!!!!!!!!!!! *Click.*

~ ~ ~ ~ ~ ~ ~ ~

2 p.m. Eggs, bacon, toast, fruit salad, pastries.

4 p.m. Ahhh...feet up, looking over today's mail, sipping my iced café you-know-what. Ben is in the living room practicing chords on his guitar and humming. Every now and then he stops, and I hear him say things like "Oh, yeah!" or "Take that!" Pretty sexy, I must say.

Dylan and his girlfriend are getting ready to meet up with friends. In my hand is the first mailing from the Sisters of Our Most Merciful Lord that I've actually looked at in months. It's just a postcard, not the usual five-pound document filled with catchphrases that are all hip and now and enlightened. I mean, these are *nuns*! Shouldn't they sound more, well, nunnish?

But, refreshingly:

> *~REFLECTIONS FROM THE SISTERS OF OUR*
> *MOST PRECIOUS LORD~*
>
> *Join us at our ocean house...*
> **for a restful week of spirituality and laughter!**

Ocean house? Laughter? Hmm-m-m...maybe they *are* hip.

Ring. Ring. Beep. "It's Tink. Your message?"

"Hi, Tink! It's Adeline. Feeling better, sweetie? I thought maybe some weekend we could take a drive with the boys up the coast, maybe have a nice lunch! Call me." *Click.*

A nice lunch with our guys? Sounds so great.
Oh! What's this? A luxury resort brochure?!?

ABSOLUTELY FREE WEEKEND!
COME CHECK US OUT!
DEAR MARGE CASAWILL—

(Oh, great. Here we go again.)

IMAGINE YOURSELF AT AN UPSCALE
RESORT FOR TWO WEEKS EVERY YEAR!
THAT'S WHAT TURN-AROUND
VACATION GROUP OFFERS YOU
YEAR AFTER YEAR!
AND DOESN'T THAT SOUND BETTER
THAN WHERE YOU ARE STAYING NOW?
CALL NOW FOR YOUR FREE...

Excuse me. I BELIEVE HEAVEN IS SUPPOSED TO BE EVEN BETTER THAN A RESORT. AND CHEAPER.

They're sending this offer to my mother? She's not here anymore. *But I am.* Maybe I could…hmm…

Maybe I'm not quite the good person I used to be.

Shit. I'll check that one out with Fr. Rob. You know, ethics and crap like that.

~ ~ ~ ~ ~ ~ ~ ~

The Family Vacation Planning Guide, Part 534:

The rest of the day is spent working on my parents' business matters, Dylan's laundry, doing comfort measures for my injury, looking for my cousin's stupid sketchpad, trying NOT to think about matchmaking Little Tink or my brother with another eligible human being of marrying age, helping get a clothing and supply list ready for Dylan's summer camp counselor job coming up, thinking about and writing a few more notes for the nursing paper, having a couple of unexpected nearby friends stop by, re-looking at the travel books at the public library and my private library (The Big Chain Bookstore), going back to the auto travel place—again!—going online, asking friends, and praying to God for direction. During which time, at night, my Ben looks up from dreamily strumming his guitar and asks me a simple question:

"Why don't we all just stay here?"

Now, you may think this is a sweet gesture on his part, but what you don't know is that we've recently said, and I quote us both: "WE WILL NOT TURN THE HOUSE INTO A SUMMER RETREAT FOR EVERYONE THAT WANTS TO VISIT MAINE."

I answer him lovingly and politely. Kind of. And then apologize after he asks me why I am shouting at him and being so hostile.

I call Ali back.

Me (oozing warmth): Hi, darling! I think I found a couple of great places inland—kind of woodsy, rustic, but clean…

She: Oh, I meant to tell you! John says he doesn't want to go inland. Too buggy.

Uh-huh.

So for the remainder of the weekend, we have 38 more conversations. WHY, OH WHY, IS IT SO IMPOSSIBLE FOR TWO REASONABLY BRIGHT WOMEN WHO MANAGE TO MAKE ALL KINDS OF DECISIONS DAILY—HOURLY— EVERY MINUTE OF THEIR LIVES—TO COME UP WITH A VACATION SPOT? I MEAN, IT'S NOT LIKE IT HAS TO BE ONE OF THE WONDERS OF THE WORLD. I MEAN, *COME ON!!!!*

Oh. Apologies.

Hormones.

Ali and I continue to e-mail. I call a bunch of my friends. I even ask Dylan's girlfriend Megan if she knows of a good place ("Um, I live in Ohio. Do you mean in Ohio, Ms. Casawill?"), and I check the Internet again for vacation spots. We go back and forth from a close-to-the-beach spot in Popham, to a pricey resort in the Brunswick area, to inns in Camden. Up the coast and down the coast. Too expensive, or no availability for our vacation week.

Dylan and Megan head back Sunday, with two grocery bags of healthy food and snacks, and $40 palmed into Dylan's grateful hands, earning me extra hugs. The giveaways are a last vestige of being able to mother an almost-completely-grown child. I'll hold onto it as long as I can. Food talks. And money speaks volumes.

~ ~ ~ ~ ~ ~ ~ ~

7 p.m.

Ring. Ring. Beep. "It's Tink. Your message?"

"Hi, Mom! It's Dylan! What's up? Oh, yeah, Megan says thank you, she really had a great time in Maine. So anyway, I left a whole box of stuff I was supposed to bring back to school. In that red milk crate. And the blue pack of CDs on my dresser? I know it's a lot of stuff, but do you think you could possibly send it to me? I could probably chip in and pay, like, at least half the mailing costs. Thanks, Mom! I love you!" *Click.*

Oh, he is *such* a sweet boy!

Before I go back to check vacation spots online, I briefly hit the mail pile on the kitchen table that I haven't sorted through yet.

~REFLECTIONS FROM THE SISTERS OF OUR MOST PRECIOUS LORD~
CAN YOU HEAR THE CALL OF OUR LORD IN THE SILENCE OF THE TREES, THE SMILES OF YOUR SISTERS, THE WARMTH OF THE COMMUNITY? COME SEE FOR YOURSELF DURING OUR TRANSITION INTO—

Ugh. I don't have time to look through a three-inch-thick mailing.

I toss it.

The phone rings, blissfully taking me away from mail detail.

Ali: Mom, what should we do? I'm exhausted. I just want to find a nice place for a few days…

Me (sympathetically): I know, honey. It shouldn't be so hard to find a place. I'll keep looking.

What was that about the "silence of the trees, the smiles of your Sisters?" Ahhh. Sounds heavenly.

I am at the computer again. Ben walks through.

He: Nothing yet?

Me: No. Plus, I have to remember to cancel that other place before it's too late.

He: Other place?

Me: You know, the place my friend recommended on the water in Edgecomb, wherever that is. Close to Wiscasset, I think. Not far from Boothbay...attractive, price not bad, full gourmet breakfast included...Uh...

I have trouble explaining to him why we haven't wanted to stay there. I can't remember. Neither can Ali when I remind her we still had a reservation. And now she's screaming with joy.

She: I'LL LOOK IT UP AND CALL YOU BACK!

The shout of which was NOTHING compared to the next call from her, which can be heard from my phone in Maine to the cornfields of Iowa:

IT'S PERFECT!!!!!!!!!!!!!!!!!!!!!!!! WHY WERE WE LOOKING AT OTHER PLACES?!?!?!?!?!?!?! I LOVE IT!!!!!!!!!!!!!!!!!!!!!!!!!!!!!!!!!!! !!!!!!!!! YOU ARE AMAZING, MOM!!!

Ah-h-h...Mommy points.

To: Tink@maine.com

From: FrRob@StPeter.org

Tink,

Let me try to answer at least one of your ethical/spiritual dilemmas this way: You have had so many changes—your mother's death, your youngest in college, a relationship with Ben (a blessing, but always an adjustment)—that you need to give yourself plenty of time for big decisions. So for now, I would definitely hold off on buying that purple-and-blue Coach purselet.

Yours in peace,

Fr. Rob

{CHAPTER 38}

In which our hero plans to ask the age-old question: Who am I?

It's Monday morning.

I listen to the first voicemail of my workday.

"Tink, this is Marissa calling from the Southern New Hampshire division of New England In-Network Physical Therapy. Your doctor's office referred you, and we did get your message about your work schedule. But unfortunately, none of our therapists can stay late enough to accommodate you after work. Maybe your employer can let you out earlier? Anyway, we'll plan on seeing you at the rescheduled time. The only other place I know of where our PTs have evening hours is in Massachusetts. But if you want, we can give you a referral to them. They're in Worcester, Mass."

Um, no.

"It's about another hour to an hour and a half south of here. Would that help?"

No.

"Hey, why don't I go ahead and book you with them?"

NO!

"I can get you in tomorrow at two thirty."

NO, NO, NO!!!

"Call me back. 603-555-0199. Thanks! Have a great day!" *Click.*

OK, so I now have an appointment that's ridiculous, but at least I finally have a correct phone number.

I call them back.

"You have reached the office of the Southern New Hampshire

division of New England In-Network Physical Therapy. Please listen carefully to the following automated options, as our menu has recently changed. If this is an emergency, please hang up and dial nine-one-one. If you are calling for an initial appointment, please press one. If you are calling about a prescription, please press two. If you are calling for medical records, please press three. If you are calling to order adaptive equipment, please press four. If you are calling for test results, please press five…"

Oh, come on.

"…If you need to reschedule an existing appointment, please press nine, leave a message at the tone, and someone will call you back within forty-eight hours."

Forty-eight hours?!?

…deep breath…

"Otherwise, here are additional automated options: For directions to our In-Network New Hampshire Physical Therapy office, press—" *Slam!*

That peace and mantra stuff is really working.

Note to Self: Ask Fr. Rob if extra Hail Marys will help, in general.

I take 20 minutes to do some online research for my nursing paper. It's actually going well. I can get it done, even when everything's so crazy, if I just persevere. Pretty excited about it. Need to pull some stats from clinic records. In those 20 minutes, a huge accumulation of tasks has come in. That's OK, I can do this. I immerse myself in them, one by one.

~ ~ ~ ~ ~ ~ ~ ~

To: KatrinkaC@MeHosp.org

From: MyersE@MeHosp.org

Tink, while Gloria's on vacation, Rita from the third floor is helping out. Are you getting all your work done? Check with Rita, OK? Also, please revamp your appointments so you can get to the new daily afternoon Mission and Motives in Medicine meeting.

P.S.—Feeling better? Good!

%*#&)&%)&(*()((**%%$^!!@@#!!!

Note to Self: Or extra Our Fathers.

Buzz. Buzz. Beep. "You've reached the voicemail for Katrinka Casawill at the Outpatient Clinic. Please leave a detailed message and I will return your call. For the Prescription Refill line, press four. For emergencies, press zero."

"Tink, it's Hannah at your doctor's. Um, the doctor showed your X-rays to an orthopedic doc here, and he thinks you'll also need some deep tissue work on your back. Call me to set it up. He says it probably won't be covered by your insurance company, but he thinks it will really help a lot. Ninety dollars per session—probably two sessions per week, maybe twelve to fifteen sessions to start. Call me. 555-0170. I'll give you some names." *Click.*

I look over at Peggy's empty chair. She called in sick this morning, a dental emergency. Ouch. Poor Peggy. Sounds like she'll be out several days recovering from oral surgery. I feel so bad for her. She's such a sweetie. It's really unusual for her to be out. She's so healthy and dependable, she almost never misses work. She must anticipate a difficult recovery. As long as I'm going to have to shell out hundreds, maybe thousands of dollars for treatments my insurer doesn't cover, what's another $50? I pick up the phone and call the local florist and send her a small delivery of fresh flowers. That'll cheer her up.

~ ~ ~ ~ ~ ~ ~ ~

I leave work late again, knowing Ben will have to work even later to finish all his paperwork. As I reach for the car keys in my coat pocket, I pull out a note I grabbed from the table this morning.

Tink—
Can you pick up soap and paper towels next time
you go to the store? And some bathroom cleanser?
Love you!
Ben
P.S.—Tuna salad and soup tonight?

Bathroom cleanser, paper towels, soap…see why I'm crazy about him? Not that he really cares about the bathrooms the way I do, that they're clean and beautiful. But he does get that it means something to me. We even have candles around our bathroom, pretty ones and all.

I get into my car, which is somehow reminding me of our kitchen table. Bit by bit, more of a dumping ground for food wrappers, junk mail, miscellaneous trash, and expired coupons. Why do I clip them in the first place? I never remember to take them into the store.

On the way home, I take a diversion, stopping at Dad's assisted living place. I sit at the supper table with him and his buddies and chat and give them each a hug before I leave. Then I remember to go to the grocery store.

It's a trafficky drive to get there. Slower, because a lot of the drivers on the road seem to have very important cell phone calls to make. Almost got rammed into, like, a billion times.

Hang up, people.

Damn.

Home. Yay!

I'm fixing supper, opening cans of tuna, washing and chopping celery, preparing the Ramen soup, and emptying the rest of the groceries. I keep losing track of what I'm doing and then re-rinse my hands between tasks.

Note to God:

What is it with men, anyway?!? I got the paper towels. OK, the cheaper brand, but SO WHAT? Same idea. But the soap? What the heck is his complaint with a soap? "Moisturizing?" I say. "They're *all* moisturizing. That is NOT 'girlie soap,' for God's sake. We've discussed this before. It's *advertising*. What do you want the label to say? 'Will rot the living hell out of your hands in just ten washings'?!?"

At least the tuna salad looks good. And the soup.

I'm really neurotic about food freshness, a gift passed on from my mother that I'm both annoyed with and proud of. I mean, no one has ever gotten sick from anything that came out of my kitchen. That I know of.

Me: Ben, does this tuna taste OK to you?

Ben: Yup.

Me: Doesn't it seem a little fishy-tasting?

Ben: It's tuna.

Me: You have to be careful with tuna, you know.

I have visions of bulging cans, a la old-time black-and-white newsreels, people sick and dying. Last century's tuna scare, per my mom's account of it.

Ben: It's fine. Are you feeling OK? C'mere. You look tired. You've been running around a lot today.

Me: I'm tired, everything's a mess, and you criticized the soap I got.

Ben: Are you gonna eat more tuna or is it up for grabs?

Me: It's *all* moisturizing soap now!

Ben: Good tuna, babe!

{*Chapter 38*}

After supper and dishes, I look for Lorraine's damned sketchpad, retracing all her steps in the house, from the chaise lounge in the garden to the ancient hot tub out back that's always needing repair. I'm mentally adding up how much time I have spent looking around for her sketchpad. I mean, I am trying to recover from an accident. I grab the cold pack from the freezer.

Ring. Ring. Beep. "It's Tink. You know what to do."

"Hi, Aunt T! It's Little T! How are you? Hey—my friends and I are really enjoying your blog!! Just wondering—um, are you remembering to check it and write in it, like, pretty much every day? My old friend Sherrie from Arizona—Remember? We were in *Annie* when we were kids years ago. Says she wrote to you and hasn't heard back yet. Although she totally needs to chill out a little, you know? She wants to go to Europe to meet this guy she's "seeing" on the Internet. So I don't know if you're able to, like, get to it tonight, but she said she'd keep checking it for your advice. Thanks! Love you!!! Bye! Oh, wait! Almost forgot! I talked to Lorraine today. She says to tell you she found her sketchpad! In a box of Gaga's linens she took home with her. Love ya, Aunt T! Mwahhh! Gotta run." *Click.*

The phone rings again, but I am letting it go. No way am I going to get that cold pack in place all over again. I'm starting to feel like a contortionist with packs and positions. Nothing quite fits my body, my injuries, and my furniture.

Ring. Ring. Beep. "It's Tink. You know what to do."

"Tink. It's Richard. Just thinking about when we were kids. Uh, Tink, *achhh.* I hate to even ask you, with all you have going on. I… ah…I was going to ask if you could make Mom's famous lasagna for me sometime? I was thinking about coming up Saturday night to see you and Ben. Not for lasagna. Did Ben tell you we've been talking

about taking a camping trip this summer? Call me when you can."
Click.

Lasagna?

Camping trip? No, Ben didn't tell me anything about that. Oh, well. Boy stuff. Even if he did tell me about a camping trip, I probably wouldn't bother to listen. Now, *lasagna* I could be talked into.

I rotate my packs to different areas. I'm exhausted.

Hot pack. Cold pack.

Young pack. Old pack.

I'm so tired, I've turned into Dr. Seuss.

bills tonite!!!!! pick up more fr/veg tomor.—
energy food!!

What happens next is a little weird and kind of creepy. Ben's phone rings. He's asleep in front of the TV. And I hear a, well, *sultry* voice on his answering machine:

"Hey—it's Jordan. Call me."

Jordan?

OK, remember how he doesn't have to tell me everything?

WHO THE HELL IS JORDAN?

Wait. Maybe it's not even the right number. I mean, she didn't even say his name.

I could just ask him. No. We are our own individuals and I trust him completely. I'm sure it was a mistake, anyway. I'll put it out of my mind. Right now.

Ring. Ring. Beep. "It's Tink. You know what you can do."

"Tink? It's Lorraine. Listen, I think it's great you're doing an advice blog, but a few of my artist friends are a little irritated you're not answering them. You know, you really can't start something like that if you're not…"

Jordan? What kind of name is Jordan?

"…and that will probably be good for your back, too. Take your mind off your discomfort. If you're having any…"

JORDAN?

"…put my feet up and relax a little. I had a very difficult…"

…better be a wrong number with that sexy, throaty voice.

"…a broken pinkie nail, then I couldn't find the right kind of cinnamon rolls for my daughter and well, you know—stress!!!" *Click.*

I just can't do one more thing tonight. I have got to clear my mind and get some sleep.

The phone rings. It's my dad. He wants to know how to get the music out of "That thing, that thing there! That I'm pointing to!" I could call the front desk at Gorgeous Ageless Gardens and get someone to go to his room to *assist* him, as in *assisted* living. But I think what he really needs is a hug from me. Even though I stopped by earlier. And Ben is now snoring downstairs. He'll be that way for a while. So I pop the herbal heat pack pillow thingie around my neck (I love that spicy, slightly floral/herb smell), get in the car, and go over there for a few minutes. I return home an hour and a half later, after hugs and talk and a few tears—mine, not his—and the knowledge that his radio is turned on just right to his favorite classical music station. And he is comfortable in bed.

And now we can both sleep.

But in the morning, I'm going to ask Ben who Jordan is. Skillfully and calmly.

{Chapter 39}

Battle fatigue, an impulsive outburst, and some unexpected results.

In the morning, I go in to work extra early to work on the nursing paper, and also to be able to leave earlier in the afternoon for my PT appointment. I'll have to miss the Respect Improvement Initiative Committee meeting this afternoon. Fuck it.

I don't get a chance to ask Ben about that call. He probably hasn't even played it back yet and will be just as surprised as I was to hear it. The more I think about it, the more I think it wasn't even the right number. I mean, these things happen all the time.

~ ~ ~ ~ ~ ~ ~ ~ ~

I drive home fighting sleep, the highway passing in a blur. Open the window, close the window, open it, swing my arms and legs to perk myself up, no help. I stop twice for old, stale tangy gas-station coffee, completely gross, just to stay awake. It works. The indigestion alone keeps me alert.

Later, at home, now wide awake enough to work a 24, I look over the new PT instructions. Well, here we go. Cup of tea in hand, I tackle the directions. I'll just fit in this new "homework" between visits to Dad, paying bills, cooking, and knitting a new house with a larger kitchen table. Oh, and the blog. Maybe later.

```
Home PT—
—Warm packs x 20 min. to upper back/shoulders/neck
—Exercises on following pages as tolerated
—No more than am't indicated, 1 to 2 minutes' rest
   between segments
—Follow with cold pack x 20 minutes
—Please track level of pain throughout each day
   (use log provided)
```

(*No, I'm not doing that. It's bullshit. I mean, I hurt all the time.*)

```
—Wait re home traction—we'll talk about it later. Go easy.
—Call if questions
~Louise
```

Yeah, Louise sounds nice, doesn't she? Well, let me just say that when I started telling her about my single brother, she gave me the weirdest, almost, well, nasty look. I am so done with matchmaking.

She can just find a husband on her own.

Think I'll wait 'til later to try the exercises.

~ ~ ~ ~ ~ ~ ~ ~

{Chapter 39}

I have just enough time to—

HOLY. SHIT.

Well, everybody! Wow! I can't believe how many of you have written to me! Aunt Tink is so very flattered. Let's see. 2,354 comments and questions, it says. But let me get to a few, and then I have a couple of "secret messages," OK?
Here we go!

Ah! I think I know which one to start with. The idiot Little T told me about.

Dear Aunt Tink,
I met this very cool guy online and am planning to meet him in Brussels next month. He seems very kind and apparently has a really good job. He told me he owns his own company in Paris. The only thing I'm a little nervous about is he looks just like Brad Pitt. I don't mean kind of like Brad Pitt, I mean exactly like Brad Pitt...

Hel—lo! Earth to Cinderella, come in please!

...When I e-mailed him and told him that, he wrote back that it was funny I thought that, that sometimes pictures look just a little different from the actual person when you meet them. My friend tells me to be cautious, but he is SO nice! He's even renting a little cottage somewhere for us to stay in when I get there. He's really into the wilderness thing and survival and stuff. Which does sound a little weird, since he says he has to be at his office "24/7 and I mean I never get a vacation." He told me to leave my cell phone behind, that he wanted to get to know me really well without the outside world intruding. Oh, and my friend's worried because he apparently had a little trouble with the law years ago. He said it wasn't anything too serious. I mean, the laws there are so strict! They'll put you away for years for, like, traffic fines. But he's out now, and like I said, getting real successful. But anyway, what should I tell my friend so she gets off my back?
Annoyed in Arizona

Dear Annoyed,
Aunt Tink hardly knows what to say (He) to you, dear. The way I look at it, someone who can't pay (sounds like) attention to "traffic laws" might not be such a good bet (a mass murderer). Your friend is (You) right to be concerned. I mean, what if (are) you are in the car with (a complete) him and he doesn't signal properly (moron)? You can get into a lot of trouble that way! Save your (Your judgment) money, dear, and maybe think about starting a nice hobby—taking (is beyond pathetic) a dance class—or just reading a good

book! Wouldn't (Could you) that be a special (possibly be) way to honor (that desperate?) yourself? Good luck! You sound like a wonderful person.
xoxox Aunt Tink

Now, I'd like to ask all my fabulous readers to take just a half hour to sit quietly with a good book. Put your problems away for a while! You know, reading is very important.

Done. For the time being.

I start part of the PT regimen, and I get a glimpse of today's mail, which is sitting on that thing we once called our kitchen table.

YOUR *NEW*
PREMIUM POINTS CARD
HAS ARRIVED,
MARGERY CASAWILL!

I still have so many places to notify of her death. How could one woman possibly have so many credit cards?!?

cancel cr. card—look @ policy—death cert.—
need 5 copies—mail certif. w/req.—f/u call—
pay bills!!! EAT fr/veg in fridge!!!

Oh, no. I forgot to do the PT log sheet.

HOURS: 7am 8am 9am 10am...etc.

√ HURTS LIKE HELL!!! ALL THE TIME!!!

There's lots more junk mail. And, what's this cool postcard? A really colorful artsy sketch. Oh! It must be a thank you from Lorraine from when she—WHAT? It's addressed to Ben and the other side just says, "Looking forward to seeing you." Huh? And there's something that looks like an initial, but it's hard to read...an O? Q? T? F? J?

Who knows.

This does not make sense. Maybe a weird joke? Still, it is not good to mess with a perimenopausal woman.

This is Ben's late night at the clinic. I'll ask him later.

After I finish the PT exercises and cold packs, I check my blog one last time before bed.

Ben calls. He's grabbing a late supper with Don, our friend at the clinic, then he'll be home. Says he can't wait to see me. Oh, well. I'm sure that postcard is a joke, then.

I'm sitting at my computer, cold pack artfully duct-taped around my upper back—not an easy task, I might add—when it hits me.

J? J...J?!?!? Like...Jordan?!?

Oh, damn.

~~~~~~~~

Ask Aunt Tink

Personal Advice for Your Personal Problems!

post a question | review account | emails recieved 29

Dear Aunt Tink,

I'm a man in my late 50s and ever since my mother died, I feel lost. I'm trying to find a girlfriend, but so far, nothing is working out. My sister was going to set me up with a date, but something came up and it fell through. I feel so hopeless. What should I do?

R. in NH

Like I don't have problems of my own?!?!?

Dear "R,"

Is it possible your sister has been **a little busy?!?**

How about getting your pathetic ass (oh, please excuse me, readers) up here to help with Dad and the junk in the storage units, you obnoxious wuss.

Tink

P.S.—Really sorry, readers.

SEND. *There!*

Oh my God. I really need to pull myself together. Hope that was Richard who sent in that question. Yikes. That's it. More caffeine tomorrow.

As an experiment.

Gotta be scientific about this breast thing.

Call Richard…tell him I was completely kidding—sorry or similar. Or maybe I can go back onto the blog and apologize…use it as an example of how people need to take a few deep breaths before they react in anger.

Yeah. That's what I'll do.

Wait. What the—?

Ask Aunt Tink
Personal Advice for Your Personal Problems!
post a question | review account | emails recieved 32

You go, girl!
Vinnie in VT

Wow, Aunt Tink! You are awesome! Could you help me tell my sister-in-law off?
Lynn in LA

Oh, God.

I begin to type:

Special Advice to…well, you know who you are:
Aunt Tink would like to suggest you put your problem aside for a while and "take it out" another time. Remember, when you are in the midst of a difficulty, you must take care of yourself and give yourself some distance from the problem. No need to fix everything

immediately. Remember the basics. Self-care.

I should talk.
And I end with:

Aunt Tink is signing off for tonight. Feeling a bit worn out herself. Good night, everybody. AND DON'T FORGET: BRUSH AND FLOSS!

Aunt Tink, thank you for the "Special Advice!" I know it was for me! Wow! I am so flattered! I'm brushing and flossing as I write this! —Gayle in Houston

Aunt Tink—read your special advice—going to do just that my problem—put it away for the night—with a six pack. —Cory in CT

Dear Aunt Tink—I'm pretty sure you were speaking to me in your "Special Advice." Not that we're not all special, but, well, my mom always told me I was the MOST special, the smartest, the prettiest, the—

File.
Close.

EXIT.

{Chapter 40}

Katrinka revisits an aforementioned eternal question and begins a discourse on getting physical.

The next morning, I decide not to ask Ben about the phone message or the postcard from "J." I'll wait to see if he says anything. I mean, he came to bed last night so sweet and snuggly and sincere. Not at all like a man who would be, well, seeing someone else. At least that's not what his body language said.

Wow.

~ ~ ~ ~ ~ ~ ~ ~

Here's what I notice about wearing a soft collar: it's hard to tell if it's helping, because every thirty seconds or so I have to pull those tender little neck hairs out of the Velcro. Kind of cancels out the concept of relief.

To Everyone Who's *Never* Been Injured in a Car Accident:

I'll bet it sounds fun to get a massage. A while back, I tried it. It was very relaxing. But after the car accident, in which the "other guy" was DWS (Driving While Stupid), my neck, back, shoulders, arms, and, after a time, pretty much every muscle connected to every muscle that ever even *heard* of my neck, back, shoulders, and arms were seriously messed up. But enough about my suffering...and P.S.— Aunt Tink loves to receive get-well cards.

Anyway, turns out that my new massage therapist, Nancy, does amazing work with deep tissue therapy. Which means that every few minutes, just as I'm beginning to feel soothed, she does something that feels like she's about to snap a bone. Or pull a leg or arm off me. Or crush my sternum into my heart. Not that it's painful.

I walk into her office, quietly sighing and groaning from fatigue and pain.

Me: Don't kill me today.

She giggles. She's tall and slim and pretty and smiles a lot and doesn't really *look* like a serial killer.

The doctor I go to (I'll call him the Great Manipulator, not because he has a character flaw, but because he does wonderful osteopathic manipulations on me) is really motivated to fix his patients. Usually, when I go for a treatment, it's pretty straightforward. But occasionally, he has to really work at getting the tightness and kinks out. Sometimes my "whatever" (backbone, rib, fingernail) just doesn't want to give in. The other day, he tried several different moves before the task was accomplished. The guy just doesn't give up. From the next room, they must think there's a sumo wrestling contest going on. Especially since, after all the commotion, shouts of "Acchhhh!" and ""Oohhaiiii!"(and that's just what the doctor is emitting), furniture moving, banging against the walls, we emerge, smiling and shaking hands, soaking in sweat and bowing to each other.

He: One week?

Me: Yes, Doctor-san.

He gives me a different soft collar to take home and try. We give a final bow, which I am now able to do more easily.

~ ~ ~ ~ ~ ~ ~ ~

> **To: All Outpatient Staff**
> **From: KatrinkaC@MeHosp.org**

Please note that due to a partial medical leave, I will be in the office *mornings only* until further notice. Please do **not** leave urgent messages on my voicemail in the afternoons. You will need to ask another nurse to assist you.

Thanks!

Tink

Ring. Ring.

Great. Found out my short-term disability will kick in. I won't have to lose pay while I race to appointments, thereby adding to peace and gratitude.

Ring. Ring.

Ahh…I won't be receiving short-term disability for the next month because of the way my employer's paydays fall on the calendar, thereby shooting the peace and gratitude theory to hell.

2 p.m.

My beeper goes off.

I was supposed to leave the office at 1p.m. My PT appointment is at 2:15. I finally got it arranged nearby, with no time for lunch.

Beeper again. I take a look. Ext. 54435. Oh, come on.

I dial it fast on my cell phone. No answer. It goes to Gloria's voicemail. Damn. I hang up, only to see the message light on my cell phone.

"Tink? Gloria. Hey, after your appointments this afternoon, could you stop back at work? There are a few things that need to be looked at. I'll leave 'em in your mailbox. Thanks!"

{*Chapter 40*}

3:35 p.m., back at the office, sore from PT.

Buzz. Buzz. Beep. "You've reached the voicemail for Katrinka Casawill at the Outpatient Clinic. I am currently in the Clinic only part-time, so if this is urgent, dial zero and someone will assist you. For prescriptions, press four. Otherwise, leave a non-urgent message."

"Tink, it's Dr. Johnston, upstairs in Geriatric Medicine. Hey, heard you weren't feeling well. Touch of flu? Anyway, a client of mine has a batch of paperwork that needs to be done. Maybe follow-up phone calls, too. Dr. D. says you get things done pretty fast. Uh, it's just after three o'clock. I'll inter-office it down to you, so you can pick it up from your mailbox, OK? Thanks. Really appreciate it. And take care of that stomach thing or whatever it—huh? What'd you say, Joyce? Oh. An accident? Oh. Oh, sorry, Tink. I didn't realize you'd had an accident. Well, nothing contagious then. Thank God!" *Click.*

...breathe...breathe...

I glare at the phone and give it the finger. And breathe.

{CHAPTER 41}

In which we find Katrinka immersed in her workaday process, all of which exhausts and annoys her, leading her back home again for further exhaustion and annoyance and a well-deserved spiritual promise. One might suggest to our hero and to the faithful reader (that's you) that during her journey, a large whiskey sour might be in order before reading the account of her day.

Thirty-four more voicemails. Most of them are about prescription refills because there is a problem with the Refill line. When I call the Help Desk (oh, ha-ha) the line just keeps ringing. I e-mail them, and get the standard:

"A ticket number will be issued and you will hear from a Help Desk representative within forty-eight hours."

Yeah. Whatever.

Other messages?

- Gloria—letting me know Peggy will be back tomorrow. All went well with dental problem and recovery, thank God.
- A niece asks for green floral teacup and "sweet little sugar spoon that matches."
- Dr. Myers needs schedule of all my medical appointments for the next four weeks. Think I'll send entire calendar year, including social and family events, flossing schedule, details of sex life.
- Mrs. Stewartson (now in Hawaii) thinks medicine is affecting her urinary tract.
- Patient Emily: "Guess what?!? I'm pregnant. And I thought I was just coming down with a cold."—Note to self—never trust any 19-year-old…

- My mother's former medical insurance company undercharged her—she owes ten days' worth of premium on old policy—maybe give them address of cemetery?
- Ben: "Sweetheart, are you still there? I'm leaving soon for my lesson, and I might look around the music center afterwards. See you later, OK?" Hmm.
- "Hi, Tink—Becky, in the staff room. It's four o'clock. Did you know you have a ton of stuff here waiting for you? Actually had to give you two mailboxes. Don't forget Peggy's mailbox, too. And—hang on—yeah—someone's waiting to give a urine sample. I'll just tell him you'll be out soon. By the way, did I hear you're giving away teacup sets? I LOVE teacups. Let me know—hint, hint."
- *ClickClickClickClickClickClickFuckingClick.*

OK, this is all bound to get so totally better but just in case and meanwhile where the hell is that secret piece of dark chocolate oh Thank you GOD here it is.

…ahhh…breathe…melt…swallow…breathe…

To: All Outpatient Staff
From: MyersE@MeHosp.org

Please be aware that our main second floor Staff Room will be undergoing the long-awaited renovation, beginning tomorrow morning at 9 a.m.…

I am not reading this.

…Although there will be some inconvenience, we expect that when completed, the renovation will afford more efficient use of space. For the next two weeks, we can expect some amount of disorder…

I am not…

> Support staff will have moveable, temporary bins set up for the daily charts that come upstairs from Medical Records…

Oh, come on.

> Posted signs will assist you. We will also post the support staff's temporary work assignments while the 2nd and 4th floor secretaries are at the weeklong "File for Victory!" seminar in Texas.

At this point, I start laughing, so hard, and it's so good to really laugh at its ridiculousness, and oops—a little air sneaks out (and for a little bit of air, it's really quite horrid) and oh shit! OF COURSE, here comes that nice mild-mannered mannequin of a lady social worker from upstairs. Why, why, why, Lord, can I not fart in peace just ONCE?

> **To: All Staff**
>
> **From: MyersE@MeHosp.org**
>
> Please be notified that due to a report of an odd odor on the 2nd floor, Engineering has been called and will check into it.

~ ~ ~ ~ ~ ~ ~ ~

By the time I get home, I am ready to cry. Or collapse. Or both. Although I'm pretty psyched that I tabulated the clinic stats and made great progress on the nursing paper, between other tasks. It's been a lot of work, but I'm almost done. Maybe if I stay late at work a few days…

I still have to do my PT exercises tonight. I look like hell, I feel old, I smell that faint combination of antiperspirant and B.O. emitting from me, I feel greasy on my face, I probably haven't had enough fluids today, Ben is out, and the dog has peed on the kitchen floor.

It's then, at what some people call a pivotal moment, that I consider what my life is turning into, how it happened little by little, and that I have to figure out where to draw the line before it's too

late. There's such a fine line in balancing things in life, and I think, well, I'm not very good at it. I'm better at giving advice—all that self-care stuff—than taking it myself. I am so overwhelmed. Need to get… (ugh!)…*grounded*. I take a deep breath, hoping that things will improve, and begin to look through some of that stacked-up mail all over my kitchen table. One thing at a time. Just one.

Several pieces of mail have the return address of the Sisters of Our Most Precious Lord. And a postcard asks me if I might need someone to handle "estate affairs during this difficult time." My appointment as my mom's Personal Representative was recently listed in Public Notices in the local paper, so now the vultures are out and hunting.

Dozens more letters are addressed to "Ask Aunt Tink" blog readers searching for answers. I wish *I* had an Aunt Tink to talk to.

I wish Ben were here and not at his guitar lesson. Well, that's healthy for him. Maybe later, he and I can just play checkers or something quiet like that.

And maybe I should think about regularly doing something for myself. I've tried the knitting thing. That was just plain scary, producing an unevenly knitted and knotted scarf that would have been long enough to fit Bigfoot. But maybe I could take in a movie once a week, even if I have to wear my soft neck collar or bring a warm pack or mini-pillow. I close my eyes for a minute to imagine it. A place to escape, to hide away. If not within, then outside of myself, a brief protection from demands.

The dog gives a bark, startling me back to reality. Even the dog needs me. I get him a biscuit and go back to my task.

~REFLECTIONS FROM THE SISTERS OF OUR MOST PRECIOUS LORD~

To all Sisters and Associates,

Please take some reflective, prayerful time to comment on the recent shift in our expression of devotion to our God-given mission. In the calm of the convent, in the quiet of reflection, are we:

˜still accessible to each other?

˜effectively communicating?

˜holding true to our commitment to our Lord?

YOUR INPUT IS CRUCIAL!

Please use the back of this "green" recycled postcard mailing, fold it over and mail it back for our further discernment.

Yours in Christ,

Sr. Mary Howard

Huh?

Ugh. I shouldn't have tossed out all those mailings without reading them. What kind of lousy Associate am I, anyway?

Oh, well. I'll just write something all loving and supportive and stuff. What was it they said in the last mailing? Something about trees? Beaches?

Dear Sisters,
Sounds great!
So many things to reflect upon—
In peace,
~Tink

Ugh. I am such a fraud.

In the distance, Little Tink's voice is coming over my answering machine singing a few lines of a funny song she's making up with a goofy accent, and I start to giggle and feel a little boost. Maybe I really can "put things away" and concentrate on life's moments of enjoyment. That's what my mom would have wanted for me. She'd probably be advising me to put all that paperwork of hers aside, too. Uh, kinda like she did.

I open the refrigerator to get some juice. The glass container slides out of my hands and crashes to the floor. I will leave the details of what followed, including what came out of my mouth, none of it related to peace and gratitude, to your imagination.

To: FrRob@StPeter.org
From: Tink@maine.com
    Dear Rob,
    I'VE HAD IT!!!

You're sure about this eternity and happiness stuff, someday, right? 'Cause if I thought this was all there is…well, things haven't exactly been rosy lately.

I miss my wonderful, sweet mom—the way she always comforted me—listened to me—sympathized.

Keep me in your prayers, OK? I have PMS. I think you know about that stuff, right?

Love,

Tink

To: Tink@maine.com

From: FrRob@StPeter.org

Tink, stay strong ☺

You are under a lot of pressure and your injury has not yet healed ☹ ☹ ☹ !

But to answer your question? Yes, there is most certainly another kind of life after this one is done. We are promised that by God. Why, I'll bet you'll see signs of that all around you if you are open to it. Your dear mother's soul goes on, in Heaven, with our Heavenly Father!

Rest tonight. I'm worried about you.

And yes, I heard about PMS. I grew up with 9 sisters, remember? If that wasn't the Lord's test, I don't know what was.

Love ☺

Fr. Rob

P.S.—I may be coming to Maine soon. Hey—you still owe me that breakfast out!!! ☺

{Chapter 42}

Dieting. Penis size. Lunch tables. Strings.

I have a "skinny" frozen dinner for supper, consisting of four pieces of cooked carrots, three string beans, nine soy beans, six bites of chicken (supposedly) the consistency of Play-Doh, possibly as much as a third cup of noodles, and a surprisingly tasty brown sauce. Ben eats cheddar cheese, peanuts, and a gin and tonic. Two, actually. I love how free he is. Doesn't even count calories. And he never gains weight. It's just nasty.

I've made a decision to ignore the mistaken phone call that Ben has never mentioned, and the "J" postcard. I don't need to invent trouble that doesn't exist.

I also decide that I will check my mother's e-mails tonight and finally, sadly, close out her e-mail account. A few nights ago, Ben sorted through some 1000+ e-mails, mostly junk, leaving me only a few dozen new ones to check. Just want to make sure there is nothing important there.

I look over the subject of a recent one:

"Decrease your appetite! Here's how!"

And I'm, like, *Wow. I don't think we'll be worrying about Mom's appetite now.*

And guess what?

Turns out it wasn't about her appetite at all. They just want to increase the size of her penis.

I never do close the account, though, because, still barely upright at my computer desk, I am just drifting off for one of those impromptu naps when I'm jostled by the answering machine.

Ring. Ring. Beep. "It's Tink. Leave a message."

"Tink? It's Dad. Daddy. You know…well, you know who I am. Was that you visiting me the other day? That was you, right, Tink? My friend here—oh, you know, the nice fellow I sit with in the dining room, he said it wasn't you, that maybe I imagined—"

I can't stand it. It's so heartbreaking. I pick up.

"Dad? Hi. It's me. Yeah. No, I was just heading to bed. No, it's OK, Dad. Yes. Uh-huh. Yes, that was me. Uh-huh. Uh-huh. Well, Dad…Dad? Dad? Listen, OK? Look, the guy at your lunch table doesn't understand everything that goes on, OK? Yeah, that's right. Uh-huh. OK, I'll tell him when I come over next time. OK, love you, Dad."

These kids…

And again, the tears begin.

~ ~ ~ ~ ~ ~ ~ ~

Ben is putting new strings on his guitar when I walk through the living room, before bed.

"Oh, good! You finally got yourself a really good set of strings," I say.

"Actually," he answers, "my guitar teacher gave them to me. Pretty nice, huh?"

"Excellent!" I say. I love free stuff.

This guitar teacher is a *very* nice guy.

{Chapter 43}

Our hero puts up with continued gatherings at the castle and listens to offers of healing from throughout the kingdom.

The next day, I'm in the car, feeling upbeat, repeating a new mantra…

I love my job — I love my life — I love my job — I love my life — I love my job — I love my —

~ ~ ~ ~ ~ ~ ~ ~

Staff meetings—beyond boring. For mental survival, most of us do tasks completely unrelated to the meeting. Of course, a few are paying attention, or pretending to. I want to run screaming from the room, but instead, I comfort myself by writing a letter to Ali. I look like I'm taking notes. I am. Notes that say, "Hi, Ali baby! How are you?" I swear I can see someone doing a cooking project behind his newspaper. And someone else is giving birth in the far corner next to an old computer that got left behind ten years ago, part of our new cost-saving HMO medical plan. Peggy is back, looking surprisingly terrific. Wow. Was that dental surgery or a vacation in St. Thomas? It'll be nice to have her gentle yet strong presence in our office again.

This morning is a *special* staff meeting. The Annual Give-Part-of-Your-Lifetime-Savings-to-Us-and-We'll-Leave-You-Alone-for-Another-Year-We-Promise drive is on. But there is also a staff member retiring.

Fifty people squished into the room, chairs wedged, like leftover junk from a garage sale stuffed into the trunk of a car headed toward the local recycling center. In dead center is a table with a store-bought "farewell" cake, a coffee pot, a dish with barbeque chips, thirteen unmatched paper plates and two dozen cups, some with Santa. And a few Batman.

Sometimes I dream about working somewhere more humane, if such a medical facility exists anymore. I just love my patients and have developed a good working relationship with literally hundreds of them, and being a part of their lives as a helper is both humbling and gratifying. But it wouldn't hurt to take a peek at the Help Wanted ads. That's it: a movie each week and maybe...a different job.

Dr. Myers begins a brief speech to the retiree being recognized. Others make stilted comments. Then the "bigger" director ties this all in with the company mission statement, which is then agonizingly, boringly presented by the BIGGEST—uh—director. Then it segues (you know—"seg-ways") into the heart of the regular business meeting, which consists of a series of PowerPoint graphs and figures...

kill self or ? take drugs before nxt staff meet.

...that no one understands or can even see through the crowded room with its awful and inconsistent lighting. The "Good Luck! We'll Miss You!" card for the honored employee continues to be not-so-discreetly signed by several staff members, the card actually being passed over the upper back and right shoulder of the Retirement Girl, while the coffee setup and the cake, in the middle of the room, sits untouched, and the business of the meeting goes on.

What if this employee got up, sliced a big piece of cake, ate it, right there, then took big hunks of it with her hands and just flung it at the administrators.

Would they even notice?

I look over at Ben. Our eyes meet, and he gives me a little wink. Ah—he knows what I'm thinking. We've talked about these scenarios all too often.

Maybe he and I will have a romantic evening together later… nothing like good sex to purge the negative energy of a bad work environment from one's system. I glance back at him, at his full lips.

Huh?

Oh.

Back to business: my note to Ali.

~ ~ ~ ~ ~ ~ ~ ~

Buzz. Buzz. Beep. "You've reached the voicemail for Katrinka Casawill at the Outpatient Clinic. I am currently in the Clinic only part-time, so if this is urgent, dial zero and someone will assist you. For prescriptions, press four. Otherwise, leave a non-urgent message."

"Tink? It's Claire, at the front desk. Is it true you have the flu? You should go home. Need the name of a holistic practitioner?" *Click.*

God.

Everyone's got an opinion. SHUT UP WITH YOURS. While recovering from the accident, friends sometimes ask how I am feeling. I used to make the mistake of telling them.

Now I say "I'm getting there" with a smile. Meanwhile, I've been subjected to everyone's well-meaning advice. Unless I become a hermit, I am pulled aside nearly every time I walked down the hallway or stand at the copy machine in our staff room.

Buzz. Buzz. Beep. "You've reached the voicemail for Katrinka Casawill at the Outpatient Clinic. I am currently…"

"Casawill? Don here. Hey, I saw you coming into the building this morning. You look a little stiff. Don't know if you'd be open to this, but I know a healer of sorts about thirty miles from here, and if you…"

Delete.

I've had offers of oils, heat treatments, cold treatments, mind-body treatments, mind over body treatments, never-mind-your-body treatments, chiropractic referrals, osteopaths, MDs, shamans, therapists of every type and size, surgeons and songsters, magicians, herbalists, neurowhatevers—all unasked for—from zealous friends who are genuinely concerned and think they have THE answer. It takes a lot of energy to tell these good folks why I'm more than happy with my own helpers. My progress, though slow, is how a 50-something body heals. But I haven't had this kind of attention since I was enormously pregnant at 19. Back then, every woman that walked past me felt a need to pat my belly, ask me if I cared about the baby's gender, and question me on my proposed infant feeding method. At the time, I remember thinking it would have been easier to just tape a big sign across me announcing the answers.

Wonder, if I do that now, post-auto-injury, if people will leave me alone. Maybe just some kind of simple sign, letting them know I'm content with the way things are going. I mean, I realize they're concerned about my back pain. Would it be confusing to people to post a sign on myself?

One that says, "Hands off. Boy or girl is fine. Breast—at least the first year!"

call Dylan—need any $? √ in w/Ali
& fam—make sure to spec. John so keep "fave"
status—

Deep, DEEP breath…

{CHAPTER 44}

In which our hero expounds on camping and cramping.

I fix a nice dinner and actually cook a real meal. The house smells of pork chops and rosemary potatoes. Ben and I eat in the dining room, with candles. OK, the kitchen table is too messy to clear off easily. It's become the depository of all things unsorted.

As we eat, we make jokes about work, and then I tell him the fabulous news: I've completed the nursing paper! Yup—I proofed it myself. I was going to ask Unflappable Peg to do it, but she seemed a little preoccupied today. She's probably just busy catching up on things, but seemed almost distant. Maybe she's having some pain. She wouldn't mention it if she was, she's so stoic. Anyway, I left the paper in Gloria's mailbox. Popped a Post-it note on it—"Call me on my cell after you read this!" I AM SO PSYCHED!!!

Ben leans over to kiss me and tells me he's so proud of me. I'd love to see Gloria's face when she opens the thick manila envelope. It should actually line me up for a merit raise at my next evaluation. And it feels great to have made a contribution to nursing practice, in my own little way.

We move on to other subjects as we enjoy each other's company. Ben talks about things from his childhood, like school and papers and tests. And exciting things, like catching fireflies (I did that, too!) and playing with snakes (no thanks to that one.) After that, he reads, and I put the dishes in the sink to soak overnight. He offers to help. I tell him to relax a while.

There's something so peaceful about the way the evening—
OH. MY. GOD.
I FORGOT ABOUT MY &$*#%*$^!
BLOG AGAIN!!!!!!!!!!

Hope none of my readers have gone off the deep end while I've been neglecting them. I mean, we're all brothers and shit like that.

I answer a few—but the last one is from a young woman who says that just because she wrote to me for advice, her boyfriend Gary (*GARY!!!!*) is now saying things will never work out between them.

She writes, "I'm so heartbroken! I work at a fruit juice processing plant and I have seriously thought of jumping into one of the vats. Except it's covered with metal mesh, and that would hurt. What should I do, Aunt Tink?"

I give her the "hang in there" answer and hope to God she doesn't do anything stupid.

Ugh. I am developing blog-head, which is worse than hat-head.

I may have to seriously rethink this whole blog thing, or maybe take Little T up on her original offer to help. If she can. I can see that if other things weren't so stressful, this might be fun.

I am shutting down my computer when Ben walks through in his boxers (very cute) and drops this note in my lap.

Tink,
Please, marry me and make me the happiest
man in the world!
And how's this idea? (Richard inspired me!)
A honeymoon camping trip!!!!
XOXOXOXOXOX
Ben

Camping?!?!?!?!? *Us* camping?!?!?

Oh, shit.
Gripping ache in my lower belly.
I'm getting cramps. Already?

~ ~ ~ ~ ~ ~ ~ ~

Men might be from Mars and all that, but they know nothing about good vacations. I'm referring to a nice hotel versus…camping.

I was a 13-year-old Girl Scout when I had my first camping experience. We piled into a couple of vans and our leaders drove us to a campsite about an hour away, where we stayed in cabins that encircled a campfire. It was pretty cushy: there were bathrooms. We didn't do a whole lot of camping, but mostly spent time in our cabins talking about boys and eating snacks we'd sneaked in. I can still smell the mixture of fresh pine air, musty mattresses, and red licorice. I have a vague recollection of several of us getting caught for something trivial, like taking off for a nearby boys' camp without asking, or hijacking a car. It's not like anyone got pregnant or anything. Although who knows? I never kept up with those girls after that.

Ring. Ring. Beep. "It's Tink. Leave a message."
"Tink? It's Richard. Hey, did Ben tell you he and I want to know if we could all go on a camping trip sometime this summer? Call me." *Click.*

Ugh! Where's the damn ibuprofen?

talk to pharm. re drugs—explain re boring staff meet.

{*Chapter 44*}

My second camping experience was at 29, married and three months pregnant with my son.

"Let's go camping," said the man of the house. With visions of a sweet log cabin dancing in my tired hormone-laden head, I agreed. We started the two-hour car ride with our eight-year-old, Ali. My parents followed in their car. At the eight-year-old's request (or maybe it was her father's idea), we drove through a fast-food place, picking up burgers, fries, milkshakes, and so on. Approximately 20 minutes after lunch was over, we pulled off the road so I could properly lose, at the side of the highway, my entire lunch. Ever the good sport, we moved along.

Memories fade, but here's what I remember: Suggesting we ask someone for directions. Suggesting again we ask someone for directions. Suggesting…oh, never mind. Then putting up a tent in the dark, after many attempts at finding the campground. Eating something that was supposed to be a meal that my then-husband and my dad cooked at about 9 p.m., and gourmet it was not. Sleeping, or shall I say not sleeping, in the thinnest sleeping bag ever invented, on a thin plastic liner on the floor of the tent, little rocks and stones popping through. Every time I moved, I got stabbed anew.

Wow. Was that ever fun.

Meanwhile, my mother had taken young Ali to a nearby hotel, had a lovely dinner somewhere, and slept on a real bed. It amazes me that I went along with the whole camping thing and that I put up with it as well as I did. Stubborn. It was years before I heard about something called a blow-up mattress.

OK, that was a definite cramp. And I might feel a little edgy. But not because of perimen-(and I emphasize *men*-)opause. I have other good reasons to feel this way.

Me: Ben! What's this about you and me and *Richard* and a camping trip this summer?

Ben: Uh, well, I, um…

Me: #*%@!!

Ben: Yes, well, I thought we could do something on our own and then maybe meet up with him, and—

Me: %^*#%#%!!!!!!!!!

Ben: But it's your brother. We love your brother.

Me: *$#&$#&^%$(#%@&%$*$#&%$*^%!!!!!!!!!!!!!!!!!!!!!

Ben: OK, well then, just think it over. You don't have to decide today.

{*Chapter 44*}

~ ~ ~ ~ ~ ~ ~ ~

Oh, shit.

I just discovered there are worse things than having pads with wings.

And that would be…um…having no pads at all. At 11 p.m. On a Sunday night. In suburban (aka "the sticks of") Maine.

With all the dozens of drawers and cabinets stuffed with junk in our old farmhouse, there is nothing. At all. Not even close. I resort to (oh, God) the clean rag bin.

~ ~ ~ ~ ~ ~ ~ ~

Even though I am not a natural camper, camping out is Ben's idea of heaven on earth. With that in mind, and with all the love I could muster, Ben and I went camping in California a few years ago in a place that could be best described as Levittown. It was the campground that hosted an awesome music festival, but it was close quarters. Very close. So close I could hear our neighbors swallowing their morning pills. One for cholesterol, one for diabetes.

There is something about overhearing intimate conversations that is disturbing. No, wait. It's…*fascinating*. Which is partly why I didn't sleep so well. The other thing might have been that the 300-degree tent we were in smelled like it had been peed on by a passing dog. Because it had.

And he wants to marry me and take me on a camping trip?!?

Me: Ben? !$(^$*^%#*$&*$(&%(^$&#&^&!!!!!!!!!!!

Stupid period.

But back to close quarters. The problem was that any time I passed another tent, I got a look at a whole new grouping of people—what they looked like, who they were with, what they were drinking, saying, cooking. It was like passing a new stage set every ten feet, me staring and feigning a friendly "hello!" when what I wanted to say was, "What's it like to be with that guy with the huge beer belly wearing that biker shirt? Do you find him *hot*?!? Does he always sweat a lot? And are your kids always bratty, or is it just because they're stuck here with you guys for a weekend?" But it was more. It was also the bathroom and shower arrangements. The outside door to the restrooms and showers had no door at all, just staggered partitions, allowing brief exposure. And the shower stalls had no curtains. There were a lot of us, so we all took turns. When my turn came, I had to sneak past a bunch of women taking showers and pretend it was business as usual. There I was, always trying to get into the last one for a little more privacy.

Now, although annoyed, I'm feeling a little less hostile. Ben holds up his old tent box in front of him. It may be my imagination, but I think he's, well, hiding behind it.

Me: I will *consider* the camping idea. Possibly with some reasonable accommodations.

And why are you cowering behind all your camping stuff? WHY?!? WHY?!? WHY!?!?!

It is possible I might have a small amount of hormonal irritability.

Oh.

Camping.

California.

After a day or so, I found that most of the women really didn't seem to care about the bathing arrangements, and believe me, these women came in all shapes and sizes. I kept thinking two things: 1)

I'm fat and cool and in your face, and 2) Ben would really like to see this. After I calmed down about the whole nudity thing, I got used to thinking it wasn't a big deal. What became the bigger deal was fighting nicely for a space to put all my stuff (my big three-tier cosmetic bag) and get a sink to myself long enough to brush my teeth and put on my makeup (20 minutes, tops) without holding up progress.

"Why don't we have a cool camper with a bathroom?" I whined, about twice a day. Or constantly. I don't remember. To which there seemed to be no answer other than, "Come on, this is camping. It's fun!"

Oh, yeah. Fun.

> **To: Tink@maine.com**
> **From: BenMan@maine.com**
>
> So—are we thinking about it?
> Ben

Huh?

I'm trying to tell my girlfriends about this dumb camping trip we had! Jeez!

OK. Yeah. So I found myself running to each music event about 100 yards and two minutes behind the rest of our little group of friends all day and all night long, mostly due to the bathroom situation. I was probably not a good sport, overall. But I did see some very lovely naked women of all types and shapes and perhaps appreciated my own body in a new way, also. Ben and I even went swimming, naked, in the South Yuba River, a delight that I will never forget and a cure for impending heatstroke on a particularly sauna-like day. It was probably life-saving. It's never a good idea to push your body's thermostat up to beyond-Sahara-desert level on a hike, especially when we "health professionals" had neglected to take water bottles with us. I was both eager and filled with anxiety about shedding my clothes in the river. Ben assured me it was OK to be naked there, and then he came very close to me and we hugged and kissed and he provided a welcome shield to a bathing-suited batch who swam by.

After that weekend, we drove to a fantastic inn on the northern California coast, where I rediscovered Ben, camping notwithstanding.

So, maybe I'll tell Ben it'll be OK to go. I'm just too overwhelmed to argue.

…feeling the peacefulness now…deep breath…ahhh…

> **To: Tink@maine.com**
> **From: RichardC@NHschool.org**
>
> Tink—So, I'll just need to know by the weekend how much tent space to reserve. Did you guys decide to go on the family honeymoon campout? Ben said he thinks you're really excited about it! But we need to reserve in advance.
>
> Richard
>
> P.S.—Turns out my older daughter would like a teacup from Gaga's collection. Can you set one aside next time you go?

Me: %^$&##&%#*^$*^$*%#*^$*$*^$#!^$&$!!!

BEN!!!!!!!!!!!!!!!! Did you think *all along* you could talk me into doing this crappy campout idea and make it "**the honeymoon**"?!? With my brother going along with us?!? And can you PLEASE go out to the store

right now and get me some dark chocolate? I have my p–

He doesn't even wait for me to finish the sentence and I hear
his car heading out the driveway. Smart guy.

{CHAPTER 45}

Paper and plant life.

Several days pass. I'm having my period, and even though I have cramps, I no longer feel reasons, justified or otherwise, to strangle innocent people.

I leave a voicemail for Gloria asking if she's looked at the packet I left for her in her mailbox, as I haven't seen her in days, other than her shadow flying out the door heading toward a meeting or whatever.

And then around noon, I get an e-mail from her saying she hasn't even had a chance to sort through anything in her mailbox other than urgent patient requests.

But at the end of the day, after I come back from my team meeting, there's a pretty blue envelope on my desk with my name on it, in Gloria's handwriting. I snatch it up to take with me, so I can savor the moment. I'm proud of myself.

I head home from work, knowing that Ben will be on his way home shortly. Earlier, he mentioned maybe we'd send out for pizza, which sounds really good after a long day. I'll make a nice salad to go with it.

It's so busy at rush hour. It seems like more and more cars are on the road all the time. I keep eyeing the blue envelope sticking out of my purse.

Oh, what the heck. There's a red light up ahead, with a huge string of traffic leading up to it. I'll just sneak a look at Gloria's note when I stop.

OK. No one will be moving at this light for at least four minutes.

"Tink, It's hard to find the words…"

Oh, this is great. All that work was worth it.

"…to say how completely lame I feel for forgetting to tell you…"

Oh, gosh, she's worried about the delayed thanks? So sweet.

"…that Peggy also volunteered…"

Huh?

"…to do the nursing paper, and we just assumed…"

What?!? Nice, kind, steady Unflappable Peg?!?

"…that you'd be too busy with all your medical treatments…"

Peggy? My officemate who was just out recovering from dental problems?!?

"…and, well, it turned out that last week when Peggy was out, she had some extra time on her hands and called me and suggested it, and really—I think you'll like what she wrote. It's pretty awesome! But I really appreciate that you…"

The light turns green.

I give my eyes, brimming with tears, a quick wipe with the back of my hand and drive on home, as it dawns on me that Peggy's dental emergency was—oh, God. Did she plan this all along? She knew I was working on the paper. How could she?

At the next light, I pop a quick voicemail onto Ben's work phone, giving him the brief version. I'm so angry and hurt.

But then I realize it's only a paper. Ben and I have a good life. We have each other, which is much more important than a stupid nursing paper. And I'll have to figure out a way to tell Gloria she's a lousy supervisor to have let this happen. And tell Peggy I hate her. In a tactful way. After all, I have to sit nine feet and something inches away from her every weekday. One thing for sure is I will never trust her again. And I've learned that the other side of stoicism, at least for her, is a mean streak.

Ben will be as stunned as I am, after all the work I did on that paper. I feel so awful. I thought Peggy was my friend. I don't get it.

Well, I have a three-day weekend to process this.

As I signal to turn into our driveway, I see the outside door is slightly ajar, and it looks like something's in between the doors. I'm not expecting anything. Probably another one of Ben's many computer software purchases. It's so cute the way he gets excited about all that stuff.

But as I get closer, I see…it's a beautiful potted flowering plant! Pink flowers, light, sweet smell emanating…Oh, he is just too sweet! It's gorgeous. I bring it into the kitchen and set it down and pull off the little envelope that says my na— Huh? It says "*Ben*?" Oh, man, did the florist mess up. I open it to pull out his message. Wow. I feel like a princess! And it says…it says—

For Ben—my favorite student!
See you soon.
Looking forward to the music festival.
—Jordan

WHAT?!?

I am breaking out into a cold sweat as I sink into the chair.

Two minutes later, Ben comes through the door carrying a pizza and looking amazingly calm and happy to see me. HOW COULD HE?!? I feel so betrayed. So taken in.

Et tu, Ben?!?

"Hi, sweetie. That absolutely sucks about the nursing paper. Those *idiots*," he says, and pops a kiss on top of my head. I back away.

"Who's Jordan?" I ask, trying to keep my voice under hysteria level.

"Jordan? Oh—my guitar teacher. Why?"

I nod toward the plant.

"Why?" he asks again.

I hand—OK, shove—the little white card at him.

"Huh. Weird," he says, and goes over to get two dinner plates from the cabinet.

"JORDAN? JORDAN'S A WOMAN AND SHE'S YOUR GUITAR TEACHER?!?" I shriek.

"Uh—yeah. Why?" he asks, all innocent.

I'm starting to remember the plans to strangle someone and now I know who.

"She sends you a plant, she buys you strings, she leaves you sexy-sounding messages, and she's taking you to a music festival? And you wonder why I'm asking?" I snap.

"Well," he says, calmly, "I don't know what this plant is about. But I don't think she sounds sexy, do you? Huh, Tink?"

"SHE'S AFTER YOU, YOU BIG DOPE!!! DO YOU LIKE HER," I scream, "MORE THAN ME?"

He is totally unfazed. I hate that.

He sits down in front of me. He takes a deep breath.

"Look," he begins. "Jordan's a great guitar teacher. One of the best. But she's a little flaky. Maybe she thought I was available and she likes older hippies or something."

I glare at him.

"She doesn't know we live together?"

"No," he says, "Why would she?"

"Well, you better clear this up with her because—independence and maturity and all that crap aside—I will KILL YOU if you EVER EVEN THINK about cheating on me and you'd better tell her we live together and it'll be a cold day in hell before you'll go to a music festival with her AND GET THAT DAMNED PLANT OUT OF HERE BEFORE I TAKE A MATCH TO IT!"

And I stomp out of the room because I'm so secure and mature and everything.

"Want some pizza?" he calls out after me.

~ ~ ~ ~ ~ ~ ~ ~

Later, I take some pizza. I'm only human. And we semicommunicate. Ben is having a difficult time understanding "what the big deal is," and at the same time, I want to know what she looks like ("I don't know; she looks like a normal person"), how old she is ("I don't know, maybe 40?")…and I'm getting a lot of vague answers.

"Hair color?"

"Blondish."

"Length?!?"

"14.783 inches! What do you want from me? I don't give two shits about her except she's a really good teacher and YOU encouraged me to finally take lessons and now you're HARASSING me about it!"

I glare at him. "Do you love her?"

"I'm not even going to answer that, you lunatic!" and he leaves the room.

"FUCK YOU AND YOUR DUMB CAMPOUTS AND YOUR SKINNY, BIG-BREASTED LONG-HAIRED HIPPIE GUITAR TEACHER AND YOUR NINETEEN SIXTIES NUDITY!" I scream after him, wondering if I've truly crossed into a very idiotic place.

So. Our first real fight. Fine.

And I drown my misery in two more pieces of pizza, carry the damned plant outside and shove it onto the dirt next to the garbage bins, feeling a pinch in my sore back, go inside, and eventually go to bed, where Ben is annoyingly relaxed and snoring.

I'm tempted to poke him—hard—but I manage to overcome the urge and eventually, after some tears, fall asleep.

{Chapter 46}

In which Katrinka continues as the sympathetic
and possibly pathetic character in a love saga.

Saturday.

Ben's up and gone by the time I get up. I look at the clock and can't believe how late I slept. Rage really takes a lot outta you.

He's left a note saying he's gone to his guitar lesson with his "excellent teacher whom I DON'T love" (good for him—using correct English, at least) and that he'll drop a hint that he has to rush home to see his fiancée. He'd better do more than drop a hint, or I'll drop more than a hint on his…well…OK, it sounds like he's being sincere. Especially since he writes, "P.S.—I'll show you later how much I love you, you adorable nutcase."

I make a quick piece of toast and some tea, and sift through yesterday's leftover mail, mostly addressed to my mother.

From an academic group she once belonged to:

****

THE DEADLINE IS APPROACHING!
WON'T YOU RENEW YOUR
MEMBERSHIP?

****

And from the college newsletter she'd written for—a column called "The Professor's Corner"—asking her to renew her annual donation to help defray the cost of publishing it:

> ********************************
>
> # WE WANT YOU BACK!
>
> ********************************

So do I!

And from a church organization:

> ## MARGE CASAWILL!
> ## PREPARE FOR AN EASTER
> ## CELEBRATION
> ## YOU'LL NEVER FORGET!
> ## ~ *a true Transformation* ~

Oh, they have no idea…

I can't stand it. With a heavy, achy pang somewhere between my throat and my chest, I take a shower and put on jeans and a T-shirt. Feeling more settled, I leave Ben a note, and head out to do some errands, and who knows? Maybe I'll go ahead and take in a matinee.

Driving down Main Street with my iced café mocha, I pass by

the music center—oh, there's Ben!—next to his car. He must have just come out of the studio. Why is he just standing there like a — WHAT?!? There is this—this *woman*—laughing and leaning toward him and touching his arm and I keep driving because if I don't, I will have to kill them both in front of God and everyone and he'd better have a good excuse for standing there with her and not strumming a guitar at the same time.

OK. I have to go back. And by the time I turn around and drive into the parking lot, he's getting in his car and she's gone and through our windows I ask him (although it could be perceived as verbally assaulting him): "WHAT THE HELL WAS THAT ABOUT, BEN?!?"

And as I question him, it occurs to me: He doesn't see it. He doesn't get it. She may be flirting with him, but he really, really doesn't get it.

I mumble that I am now going to have some "alone" time at the movies, and he gets out of his car and comes around to hug me and sweetly says (the prick): "Good for you, sweetie."

~ ~ ~ ~ ~ ~ ~ ~

Back home, it's well past suppertime. Which doesn't matter to me, since I ate a bin of popcorn the size of an SUV.

Ben is watching TV, but when he sees me, he jumps up and comes over and puts his arms around me.

"It's OK, it really is, sweetie. I only love *you*," he says, gently rubbing my back while he's hugging me.

Well, OK.

It's actually very welcome.

As opposed to the news we hear, just moments later when Ben listens to his answering machine, that his Uncle Jeff, Aunt Cindy, and their two German shepherds are passing through our area tomorrow on their every-five-year trip and hope it's OK to "camp out" in our house for a few days and that they may need to connect with a local doctor (do we know of a homeopath?) regarding an itchy rash Aunt Cindy has that seems to be getting worse and now the dogs are itching as well and do we know of a homeopathic vet also and they are not sure if the diarrhea is related or not.

Somehow, I am not thinking PEACE.

I can't even discuss this with Ben tonight. I can't hear that these were the people who lovingly took him in not once, but twice, in his younger years, when he was experiencing personal crises and felt all alone in the world.

Damn.

I pick up the rest of the unopened mail and go upstairs, passing my computer.

Oh, no. My blog is popping up.

{CHAPTER 47}

Katrinka falls prey to her own fatigue and fury.

Ask Aunt Tink

Personal Advice for Your Personal Problems!

post a question | review account | emails recieved 19

"Jennifer" wants to know if I think good manners are still important. "Ray" asks if he should offer to pay for the tickets at the movies now that he and his girlfriend are living together. And *Gary* is wondering how old I am and if I would consider dating a younger man.

Holy shit. Why? Why? Why? I cannot do this right now. I feel like I'm about to crumble. Love and peace? Right. I am so mixed-up.

I think about Little Tink, such a sweetie, so innocently giving me one more thing to do. In her need to connect, she trusted me, and yes, I was happy to do it, but God! I am right on the edge of insanity. Desperately need to decompress. What else have I forgotten or neglected lately that I don't even remember? Like the Associate mailings. I feel so guilty, like I'm ignoring the really important things. I'm not even sure what's important anymore, though in the back of my mind, I think going to that chick flick earlier may well have given me a couple of hours of real peace.

And this weekend, I'm going to get some things completed once and for all.

Yeah, well…

Reply.

You know what? *No.*

Minimize.

I'll get back to it later.

Maybe I will try to close my mother's e-mail account again tonight. Maybe I really can finish it. I feel so emotional about it, like I'm shutting off one more thing that was a part of her.

Turning back to my own unopened e-mails (I should just go to bed), I continue to look them over, deleting most.

What? What the—

From my mom's bank, which I'd e-mailed to notify them of her death, even attaching scanned copies of all the proper "proof" to close her account:

> **DEAR MARGERY CASAWILL,**
>
> **AS YOU HAVE REQUESTED, WE HAVE CANCELLED YOUR ACCOUNT. OUR RECORDS SHOW YOU HAVE BEEN A VALUED CUSTOMER FOR OVER 20 YEARS, AND WE HOPE WE CAN SOMEDAY WELCOME YOU BACK AGAIN AS A CARDHOLDER.**
>
> **PLEASE KNOW THAT YOU WILL ALWAYS BE AN IMPORTANT PART OF THE YOURBANK FAMILY. PLEASE FEEL FREE TO CONTACT OUR STAFF OF PROFESSIONAL CUSTOMER SERVICE REPRESENTATIVES ANYTIME.**
>
> **SINCERELY,**
>
> **YOURBANK CUSTOMER SERVICE DEPARTMENT**

I can't fucking believe this.

It is beyond cruel. And I am beyond screaming. I—well, I'm too upset to know what I am. Feeling wounded over the nursing paper, then the blow-up with Ben…and now this?

Minimize.

…*breathe, dammit…*

Open Word.

Nah…

Minimize.

Oh, fuck it.

Open Word.

Shit.

Minimize.

I'm trying to ignore a cramp, not very successfully, as it grabs me.

And now…I feel a certain, well, strength emerge from within my soul.

Open.

Dear IDIOTS!!!
It is beyond comprehension that I should even answer you! Just who thinks up this shit?!?
GO FUCK YOURSELVES.
Sincerely yours,
Tink Casawill

Oh, it would feel SO good to actually send it off to them, but I'm suddenly almost too tired to care.

Copy.

I can barely keep my eyes open…ugh…

Paste.

Minimize.

I gently ponder this as a haze falls over me and…peace…at last?…breat—…I suddenly am aware of hearing a voice…

"Tink, come to bed, sweetie!"

…as I catch myself falling toward the computer in one of those nod-offs of exhaustion, bracing my fall with my hands on the keyboard.

Crap. Hope I didn't break something.

Did I actually send that to YourBank? Hmm. No, probably not. Think I just minimized it. Too tired to figure it out.

And if I did send it to YourBank, too bad. It'll just go to some nonperson anyway.

File.

Close.

Exit.

Bed.

{CHAPTER 48}

The proverbial train leaves the station and picks up speed, with our hero on board.

Maybe it was just a matter of time.

Sunday morning. A new start.

Taking a hint from my departed mom in my mind's ear, I go to the kitchen and put on a kettle of tea, balancing the herbal warm pack around my neck. I know that behind the half-boxfuls of wheat crackers and five cans of formerly mixed nuts, now only peanuts left, all the good ones gone, I have a little pack of English digestive biscuits hidden away—my secret to relaxing. A cup of tea, a little biscuit, maybe I'll even treat myself to a girl movie on TV. Sandra Bullock. Or Julia Roberts. Decadent for a Sunday morning.

"You deserve it, Tink!" I hear my mom tell me from afar.

I know. I have excellent hearing.

I'm pouring boiling water into the mug when the phone starts ringing.

Ring. Ring. Beep. ""It's Tink. Leave a message."

"Aunt Tink?? Are you OK?? It's Little Tink. Um…please call me. I'm really worried about you—you know…the blog. I mean… oh (sniff), I feel so bad that I started all this! Oh (sniff, cough), Aunt Tink!!" *Click.*

Oh…she's so sensitive. What a sweetie. Finally, someone realizes the stress I've been under, the discomfort, the—

Ring. Ring. Beep. "It's Tink. Leave a message."

"Tink? Richard. Great work. Now I'll never get a date." *Click.*

Jeez. What's with *him*?

Ring. Ring. Beep. "It's Tink. Leave a message."

"Tink? It's Lorraine. What's going on? Call me. I'm really bummed out about your blog. I can barely eat my brunch!" *Click.*

Huh?

Ring. Ring. Beep. "It's Tink. Leave a message."

"Yeah. Aunt Tink? What the—?!? It's Gary. Oh, man, have you screwed up or what?!? I was really starting to, well, like, you know, admire you." *Click.*

Ugh. What is the big deal if I don't answer, like, every damn question, every day, on the blog? God.

And now Gary has my HOME PHONE NUMBER?????!!

What is he, the FBI or something?

Ben walks in. He looks nice. He always does after making up. Which included early morning words of endearment from him about me being his entire life and future and he would never, ever do anything to mess that up and he'd even change guitar teachers if that would help reassure me. And then there was the back rub and then—well, never mind. Aunt Tink likes to leave some things private, for God's sake. So what choice did I have? I told him I trusted him 100% and he should keep the teacher. A saint, that's what I am.

Ben: Sweetheart—what's going on? How come the phone keeps ringing?

Me: Dunno. Just blog junk. I'll get to it later. After I go online to check out some camping equipment.

(He's glowing. I am so smart sometimes.)

Now, for my personal tea party.

And that's when I begin to hear it.

{Chapter 49}

As the train picks up speed, our pitiable hero realizes she is heading toward an unplanned destination.

Outside, there's more than birds chirping at our country house. The noise becomes louder. There's a crowd of— of— oh, roughly 150 people. What are they doing in my yard?!?

I peek at the crowd, then back away from the window. And that's when the veil of last night's fog begins to lift. The YourBank e-mail. Minimizing. The blog…Gary's questions…OK, I was tired…then what? Then what? Think.

I review it again. Morning back rub—um, not that…review last night…

OK, I got onto my blog. Minimized it. Wrote the nasty letter to YourBank. Minimized it. I fell asleep…

Now I look outside again. Some people are holding handmade signs. One says "You go, Old Girl!" Another says "What happened to the milk of human kindness? All dried up, '*Aunt*' Tink?" Some are just shouting, "Aunt Tink!! Aunt Tink!!" One young woman is tearful, one is drinking a beer, and the front lawn—and Ben's lovely flower gardens—are being trampled. How did they find my home? Is there nothing secret in this country anymore?!? I watch this from our second-floor office window.

From our computer room…computer…*computer*…

I'm racking my brains to—

…fell forward onto…onto…the *keyboard*…

HOLY. SHIT.

{*Chapter 49*}

The damned computer.

As a couple of police cars pull up, Ben looks out.

"Cool!" he says, "Just like the sixties!" He starts to tell me about being at Woodstock, excitedly talking about the crowds, dreamily recalling his old girlfriend from back then who loved camping (*oh, great*), the people, the wild clothing and hair styles, and all that went with it, when I quietly leave the room.

~ ~ ~ ~ ~ ~ ~ ~

…inner peace…inner…peace…

I pull a small suitcase out of my closet.

From the next room, I hear Ben:

"Oh, man, I mean, it was surreal…and pretty much everyone was smoking weed…and there was this couple just *doing* it, just *doing* it right on the ground next to their car, I swear to God!…and…"

He continues to reminisce.

I am normally an agonizingly slow packer. But today, I throw a few days' worth of underwear, casual, modest clothes, and a nightgown into the bag, along with the book I'm reading. And a few old comic books.

I know.

They soothe me.

I have that tight-throat feeling as I hear a buzzing noise going off. My beeper! Of all times!

Once again, to answer or not to answer…

Shit. The clinic. I dial the number.

Me: What?!?

Dr. Myers: Tink? We're having a crisis.

Me: It's friggin' Sunday. What are you even doing there?

Dr. Myers: Long story, but the State is coming on Tuesday to audit charts and we're missing a few signed out to you.

Me: Good. Then miss them.

Dr. Myers: Tink, Respect Policy—or lack of—aside, I really need your help. Those charts are Dr. D.'s patients. He's here and those charts are nowhere to be found. Only seven out of ten are accounted for.

Holding the phone with one hand, I clumsily grab my toothbrush, toothpaste, makeup, body lotion, powder, blood pressure meds, PT equipment, pharmaceuticals, and herbal meds for my back, dumping them haphazardly into my open little suitcase.

Dr. Myers: Dr. D.'s progress notes are in those charts, from before the electronic record started, and he really needs to find them. Those charts are on the official list for the State to inspect.

…nail scissors, nail clippers (the baby kind—I highly recommend them. They do a much better job than adult clippers), nail file…

Me: Oh, well, I guess he'll just have to—

Dr. Myers: Tink, this is serious. A true crisis!

Me: Hey, I'm having my own crisis here.

…Q-Tips…

Dr. Myers: We need those charts.

Me: I don't have them, OK? I turn in my charts at the end of each day. Did you look in Medical Records downstairs? Check other people's mailboxes? Look through the stacks on the floor, the file cabinets, the—

Dr. Myers: All of it. And Dr. D. is practically having a nervous breakdown over it.

Me: Once again, "Oh, well…"

Dr. Myers: Tink, we need you to help us look for them.

Sigh.

…sunscreen, dental floss, mouthwash…

Me: Put him on the phone.

Dr. Myers: I can't. He's in the men's room. Been in there pretty much all morning.

(*Ah. Diarrhea.*)

Me: I'll see what I can do. I'll get there later or tomorrow and hopefully, have the charts ready before the State gets there Tuesday.

(*God forbid the State should know how shabby the records really are.*)

Dr. Myers: So, well, how will we know when they're found?

Me: Oh, I'll call you. On your beeper. The instant they're found.

Click.

…magazine, earrings, watch.

Suitcase zipped, I go to the top of the stairs. All of a sudden, I feel like I'm about to crumble.

"Ben?"

He's there, on his way up.

Ben: What's going on here?

Me (fighting back tears): Oh, I made a mess of things… accidentally…I was so overwhelmed, so angry, so tired, so technically stupid, I…I…

He's holding me close.

Ben: There are a lot of people outside.

I cry harder. He rubs my back as he holds me.

Ben: Want me to tell them to fuck off?

OK. I know that now I am making Ben look like a completely great, sympathetic hero in this story, even though he seemed a little lame a chapter or two ago. But it's important, for the princess ending. So just go with it.

Me: Well…What I want you to do is go to the front door in about a minute, open it, and find out what they want.
Ben: I love you.
Me: I love you more.

And with that, I retreat. I grab my little suitcase, jacket, and keys, and slink down the back stairs…as much as anyone can slink, carrying this stuff with a bad back and dragging a batch of PT equipment. Then I remember, and I drop everything and quietly hurry back up to the bathroom for one last item, making sure it's capped tightly. Ugh. You definitely don't want this stuff to spill all over. I grab a plastic bag from the pantry and pop it in, for extra protection.

A few minutes later, although this was not part of my plan for a long weekend, I'm on some side roads, heading toward my destination.

I figure my backyard neighbor will forgive me for driving over her new grass.

Great. One more gift to buy next Christmas.

{CHAPTER 50}

Our hero, nearly defeated, seeks one last thread of hope.

Bags in tow, I let myself into the motherhouse. As I smile and wave tentatively to the nun behind the counter, I sign in and feel the tears welling up and spilling down my cheeks. My signature looks almost indecipherable as the flood comes, falling on the sign-in book, and Sister Margaret quietly passes me some tissues. Just like her, so sweet, not questioning me, just giving comfort. She nods and points down the hallway, to the guest quarters.

Inside the guest suite (OK, I know it sounds luxurious, but it's very basic), there's a bed with a rudimentary thin, cream-colored bedspread, a bedside table complete with an ancient, age-stained doily, and a small TV on a low-lying dark wooden bureau. A few books on the shelves, your standard Glorious picture of Jesus, one of Mary, a simple crucifix above the bed, and a Bible on the table. A couple of lamps, a comfortable chair, and you've got yourself a place to think for a while. There's also a simple bathroom (*and clean*) and then a second bedroom on the other side of the bathroom, both rooms accessible from the small entryway.

I put down my things and begin to feel a depth of loneliness and pain coursing through me unlike any I have ever known.

I just don't know how I could have gotten so overwhelmed, so overwrought, that I had to escape this way.

I miss Ben.

And I miss my mother *so badly*. I am so heartbroken. And feeling an overwhelming and uncontrollable surge from within, I completely give in to the tightness, finally releasing tears and sobs alone, just me and my God. I cry and I cry and I cry and I cry.

Not even the Hershey bar in my purse would help.

Although it wouldn't hurt to try.

The sweet and the salty.

And I sob some more.

~ ~ ~ ~ ~ ~ ~ ~

I sit on the bed and look around again, somewhat recovered and maybe lighter.

Ring. Ring. Ri—

I pick up my cell phone.

Me: Hello?

Ben: Hi, sweetie. Where are you?

Me: I'm…I'm…I was so upset…I'm…uh, at the convent.

Ben: Oh, no! Was it the campout idea?!?

Awww.

Me: I wish it were that simple. Do you realize what I did?

Ben: Yeah. You told a few thousand people to fuck off. Good for you!

Me: But I didn't mean—

Ben: Look. These things have a way of—wait a minute. I think your beeper's going off. You left your beeper here, babe.

Me: Throw it in the trash bucket. Now. Look, I'll call you later, OK? I have to talk with someone.

And my eyes scan the wall 'til they reach the portrait of our Blessed Mother.

Me: I'll call you tonight. Just don't tell anyone where I am, OK? Change my voicemail. Say I've gone to find my true calling.

Ben: Do you still love me?

Me: Oh, *yes*. But I'm in a bunch of knots right now.

Ben: Well, call me later. Maybe I can help you untangle yourself.

Me: Call work. Tell Dr. Myers I'm off duty. The hell with the damned beeper.

(I look up at Jesus.)

Me: I mean, *darned*.

~ ~ ~ ~ ~ ~ ~ ~

Answering a knock at my door, I go and open it. I look down to find a tray with a pot of tea, a cup, and a spoon. There are a bunch of little pieces of pastry and some cut-up fruit. But no Sister. Well… OK…

I take it in and decide I can meditate on the food and tea for a while. I realize I've been here for a couple of hours and not one Sister has come to say hello.

Hope they're not pissed off that I missed, like, all of the meetings and retreats so far this year.

~ ~ ~ ~ ~ ~ ~ ~

A while later, I walk down the long, darkened, wood-lined corridor, feeling a little bit better already. It's so peaceful here. I love the faint scents of this majestic old building. I go to the bulletin board outside the dining hall, and hear the occasional minor clatter of metal utensils and porcelain dishes far off in the kitchen.

Apparently, tonight is "Box Lunch" night. Brief, written instructions remind the Sisters to pick up their supper and take it to their own rooms. There are no scheduled activities.

Most Saturday nights, Ben and I would be looking over the movie listings and trying to decide whether we'll go to a boy's movie or a girl's movie. But that was before I screwed up and sent my angry e-mail to Ask Aunt Tink readers instead of to some YourBank idiot.

I head back to the guest room to wait for suppertime.

Mixed in with the loneliness and regret, however, is a certain peacefulness. There is no one calling about what they want from my parents' belongings, no mailings or solicitations for my departed mother, no insane work demands, no—

Knock-knock.

I open the door.

"Sister Howard!" and I leap to hug her, tearful again.

As she hugs me back, she whispers "Shhhhh" and pulls back, smiles, eyes shining, pats my shoulder, then quickly moves back down the hallway before I can ask her in.

~ ~ ~ ~ ~ ~ ~ ~

Here's the thing about nuns and food. There's no nonsense. At suppertime, I get to the lineup, and quickly and quietly pick up a box lunch and drink, and just as fast, everyone has gone their own way. Weird. I mean, no "Hi. What's up?!?"

I go to my room, turn on the TV, and eat. Mmm-m-m...chicken salad (all white meat, a little lettuce, very fresh!), the good, crunchy kind of chips (40% less fat, so I can eat the whole little bagful), a crisp apple, and a BROWNIE. And *The Brady Bunch* is on reruns! I feel better already.

Before bed, I call Ben.

"If anyone asks, tell them I'm on a short retreat of sorts."

Ben's voice is warm and gentle. "I love you, Tink. I miss you."

I choke back the tears.

"I miss you," I say, "*so much.*"

And then I dial one more number.

"Hi, Dad? It's Tink."

"Tink? Tink? My daughter Tink? Oh, Tink! I'm so...ah...so..."

"Happy, Dad? Glad to hear from me?"

"Uh, well, I'm so…uh…so FULL…from dinner! They give me too much food here."

Uh-huh. Well…

"OK, Dad. Just eat as much as you want, OK? You do not have to finish everything on your plate. It's OK to leave some."

We exchange "I love you's" and hang up.

{CHAPTER 51}

Katrinka rediscovers that a "sister" is a friend.

There are none so blind as those who don't pay attention…

The next morning, I get washed and changed and head down to the dining hall. Again, I am struck by and filled with such a sense of peace here, walking through the old, wood-lined corridors. Everything is so well-kept, so old, so lovely. It has a nice, ever-so-light musty smell, from years of furniture polish used on the wood.

Just ahead of me is Sister Diana. A couple of years ago, we sang a duet during a fundraiser for the convent chapel renovation project. It was a full-habit rendition of "Sisters" from the old movie *White Christmas*—complete with Rockettes-style high kicks, which brought down the house.

I sidle up to her.

"Sister," I whisper, "as long as I'm here, wanna work up a little dance act? Maybe something a little racy?"

I giggle. She doesn't. She just takes my hand and gives it a gentle little squeeze. Oops. Maybe I offended her.

I say hi to a couple of the nuns, who simply give me a hug.

So peaceful.

Now here's a group of women who don't ask me every two seconds if "I can have the silver-plated teapot" or the "rose-and-white flowered towels" from the storage units. No pressure from anywhere. I push away the demands that try to pry their way into my brain—storage items, credit card cancellations, legal matters…even matchmaking.

Slowly, the dining room empties. I'm just about left alone, save for a nun of about 105 at another table. I got here barely in time for breakfast, as they were about to clear it away. Guess I better get here earlier tomorrow morning. Still, as the dining room is nearly empty, I am completely comfortable and even amused at sitting at a long table alone and watching at a distance as the old nun carefully brings each bite of food slowly to her mouth, never missing a beat, chewing slowly, and seemingly oblivious to all else.

I head back toward my room. As I'm passing the chapel, I stop and go in. It's lovely, though a bit overdone, what with all the ornate statues and all, gold, curvy, squiggly lines everywhere. On the way out, I glance at the chapel bulletin board just to see if there are any special masses or celebratio—

Huh?

Wh—? What's this about a *silent* order? Wow! Cool! Where would *that* be? Some far-off countr—

WHAT?!
"Holy Mother of—"

I start to shout, as a few nuns turn around from the pews and with sweet little smiles, put a single index finger to their lips and say, "Shhhhhh."

I am all turned around now. What was—? How did it—?

Oh. My. GOD.

The mailings.

The bits and pieces are flying back through my mind like the tornado scene in *The Wizard of Oz*.

I stagger back to my room. I can't believe it. I just can't believe it. Sure, the silence thus far has been, in a way, comforting. But the gentle connection I was hoping for? Now it'll all have to be in silence.

I just cannot get used to the idea.

I make the best of the shock of it all, making the bed, brushing my teeth, and putting on a little makeup. I am left with my thoughts, which are more tangled up than ever. I think about Ben. I picture him standing at the bottom of the stairs as I come down. The two of us sitting in front of the TV together. Laughing at a movie. Or making fun of all the new hospital "initiatives." I think about my mother...my father...I think about my kids and nieces and grandkids calling me, maybe leaving messages...the mailings that come for my mother, that in their ridiculousness and even humor they sting, unbeknownst to the sender. I think of my readers who rely on me for really inadequate advice and seem to take it anyway, or at least appreciate it. I think of Fr. Rob. (*Not that way.*)

I hear a knock at the door. It's Sister Howard! Who puts a finger to her lips, moving into the room past me.

"Shhhhh!" says Sister Howard. "You tell anyone I'm here and talking and I'll ban you from the Christmas party!" She goes on to tell me that the last month of silence "has been, well, HELL. If God wanted us to be silent, he wouldn't have given us our big mouths! Now, Tink, what in the world are *you* doing here?"

~ ~ ~ ~ ~ ~ ~ ~

I spill the whole thing, leaving out only my childhood, and stop intermittently to blow my nose because I'm crying so much, then run into the bathroom to make sure I don't have snot on me. (I know. I can't help it. Believe me, I've tried to overcome this.) And I include the whole thing about using "the F word" to YourBank but falling asleep at the switch and sending it, somehow, to my readership on the blog, at which point Sister Howard assures me she's heard the word "fuck" before and that I should really loosen up a little. She gives me the "God loves you just the way you are" speech and after I hug her and cry some more, I pull out one of the little bags of dark chocolate M & M's from my pocketbook and let her pick out the colors she likes. Blue and red. Which is good, since I like green the best. And yellow.

Sister Howard: Did you bring any *Archie* comics with you? Like last time?

(Leave it to her to remind me of my crisis three years ago, when I got my first-ever speeding ticket and felt wronged by the entire world and I mean, come on! I was doing 30-something in a 25-mph zone. I mean, please, people! Driving 25 makes it *less* safe, because you're going so slowly you look in everyone's windows as you're driving past their houses instead of watching the road.)

So, Sister Howard takes a *Betty and Veronica* and starts toward the door.

"By the way," she says, "not to add to your troubles, but I take it you've seen the news this morning?"

She smiles anxiously and leaves.

{Chapter 52}

Word of Katrinka's unfortunate breach of etiquette has traveled throughout the kingdom.

Sometimes things have to get worse before they get better.

A national news/tell-all channel, amongst stories of which celebrity is pregnant, which actor has been arrested for punching a reporter (I can only hope the reporter was from this same crummy station), the latest political scandal, and which fast-food chain is lying about the kind of oil it uses in its french fries, flashes pictures of my blog (at least I'd used a thin picture of myself from 20 years ago), and runs a "Where's Aunt Tink?" scandal segment. Complete with theme music.

"No one quite knows, or is saying, where Internet advice columnist 'Aunt Tink' is hiding out, following an apparently inadvertent use of foul language and harsh words to her readers. Seems the fifty-something Aunt Tink meant to send the message to a financial institution that was, quote, 'being a (BLEEPING-BLEEP)-hole,' according to a family spokesperson in her hometown in Maine."

The picture on the screen flashes to my FRONT YARD!!! where crowds still gather.

The "newscaster" (oh, *ha-ha*) continues.

"More later, as this story develops. Meanwhile, we're not the only ones who are curious. Several well-known talk-show hosts, including Ellen Degeneres and the hosts of *Good Morning America*, are attempting to contact Aunt Tink to find out what makes this gutsy middle-aged woman tick."

I shut the set off.

And there is a knock at the door.

{CHAPTER 53}

A godly mission takes on more voice,
with our hero as an innocent accomplice.

It's Sister Diana. I let her in.

"I need a little advice. And too bad about this silent thing. I just can't abide by that any longer. We all agreed to give it two months, but I swear, I am going crazy! Sometimes at night I put my face into the pillow and just scream! I mean, I'm a *singer* for goodness' sake. A SINGER!"

Knock. Knock.

We look at each other.

"The bathroom!" and she scoots.

I open the door.

Sister Bernadette doesn't even get through the doorway when she starts hugging me and saying she needs to talk and "Thank God you've come here! I know you won't tell the others we've spoken, but I need your help!"

Apparently, even nuns read advice blogs. As if it's helpful.

And then…

Oh, for God's sake, you know what happens. You've seen enough sitcoms. And it's just like that. Really. Honest.

Yeah. Well, uh…anyway…pretty soon the entire guest suite is filled with 38 nuns, each presenting herself very quietly and looking pretty guilty at first, telling me she needs to talk, then being pushed into a different closet or room, gasping as she sees others in hiding.

The only one missing is Sister Howard.

Knock. Knock.

Guess who?

Hey, look, I never promised you a surprise or clever ending, did I? I mean, I specifically said that this story will have taken you nowhere and you will have learned nothing (see page 24.)

~ ~ ~ ~ ~ ~ ~ ~

Sister Howard is at the door, looking expectantly suspicious, trying to see past me.

"Anyone in here?" she asks, eyes darting.

I am many things, but one thing I am not is a liar. God knows I've tried.

Me: Why do you ask?

She grabs my arm and pulls me closer.

She: I can't stand it anymore! You have *got* to help me figure out how to get out of this damn silence thing. Help me, Tink! I know there's got to be a way.

And then, we both hear it.

A sneeze.

Sounding eerily like Sister Diana.

Coming from the bathroom.

~ ~ ~ ~ ~ ~ ~ ~

It's been a while, in my professional work, since I've led group therapy, because my job has mostly turned into trying to outsmart insurance and pharmaceutical companies (please see earlier ranting and raving.) But this is a lively group, now gathered in the dining hall, amidst cups of tea and coffee, donuts, pretzels, and yes, M & M's, a contribution from my suitcase. As they work out the fine points of returning to their previous style, but with built-in, silent reflection hours, my cell phone buzzes. Since they're doing such a good job, I announce "Break Time!" and walk over to the doorway to answer Ben's call.

{CHAPTER 54}

In which our hero has an opportunity at true greatness in one selfless deed.

Former Fuck-up Turns Hero

"**W**hat do you know about Dr. D. and some missing charts? Apparently he's hyperventilating, and between gasps and popping eucalyptus lozenges, demanding to speak with the hospital lawyer. On a legal holiday."

For a calm guy, Ben actually sounds alarmed.

I look at the Sisters, who are now happily chatting, working on the wording for their next newsletter explaining the relevance of "spiritual discernment on matters of devotion to our Lord." They are sharing war stories about fantasies of opening a window at midnight and making wild animal noises, or praying for an emergency so they could use their voice to phone 911 for help.

I whisper to Sister Howard, walk quickly to my room, and grab my pocketbook. I'm about to shut the door when I remember, and turn back to grab that special item I'd packed in its plastic bag.

~ ~ ~ ~ ~ ~ ~ ~ ~

I arrive at the clinic 15 minutes later and let myself in with my coded badge.

As I head toward the staff room, I hear voices. I walk in.

The room is filled with the usual mess of charts, several dozen in stacks on the floor, tables, and counters. People's mailboxes also have charts squeezed in with the mail, notices, superbills, and policy handouts.

Dr. Myers—and *THE HOSPITAL ATTORNEY*—are quietly talking. I catch words like "justifiable postponement" and "failed transit of information systems" spoken in reassuring terms. They don't even see me. And there's no Dr. D., although I think I hear a faint sobbing sound from down the hallway.

I scan the room. It takes exactly seven seconds (OK, I made that up) to look at the master list, note the medical record number of the three missing charts circled in red, and find them in the mailbox labeled STUDENTS. One of them has a name similar to mine. I still can't figure out why no one EVER thinks of looking in the students' mailboxes. I mean, this is not the first time there have been charts in there, legitimately or not. I hand them to Dr. Myers, who is beyond surprised and delighted and actually comes toward me to hug me. (I back away. Respect Policy!) I slip past him and out of the room.

Now following the sound of crying, I knock on Dr. D.'s door.

It is not pretty to see a grown man so distraught. I really feel sorry for him.

Me: Found your charts, you big baby.

And I pass him the plastic bag, which, of course, contains a tightly closed bottle of Kaopectate. I mean, he pisses me off, but I'm not a total freak.

{CHAPTER 55}

Katrinka discovers that nice, happy endings sometimes get complicated.

Back at the convent, I go around to the back entrance. I don't know what's going on, but there are an awful lot of cars parked on the other side of the building, in the regular public parking lot, next door to the girls' high school. Probably a big school event. I head into the entrance where only the nuns and other cool people are allowed to go—kitchen workers, a couple of office staff, and people like me, who mess up and then make reparation and give to others and all that noble shit. I let myself in and sign back in, pleased to hear the soft din of the Sisters' chat here and there as I make my way back to my room.

After a few minutes, there is a knock at my door.

It's Sister Howard. With a cup of tea for me. And a dish of chocolate ice cream. At this rate, I may never leave. Maybe this is how they get new recruits.

We talk for a few minutes, first about my thoughts on my blog and damage control, and then the whole campout-honeymoon-with-Richard/guitar-lesson-Jordan-blow-up thing. While we are "processing" this in a "reflective" way (excuse me while I wretch, even though I love Sister Howard so much, this language thing she seems addicted to has got to go. I mean, I liked talking to her so much more yesterday when she told me she'd heard the F word.)

"Wow! Those Sisters can sure make up for lost time," I tell her, as we both begin to hear a virtual roar of voices. And I swear, the silent treatment has actually deepened some of their voices. I mean, a few of them, at this distance, sound like men.

"Sorry, Tink," she says, "I have to see what's gotten into them. It sounds like total chaos."

She opens the door, and we both see at once a veritable army of Sisters heading toward us.

A determined army of Sisters moving rapidly is a frightening sight to behold.

"They're all over the place!" shouts Sister Diana. "Cameras, trucks—this place is swarming with—"

I dodge through and race past her and the others to run downstairs to the front window, and I can't believe what I see— AGAIN!!!!!

~ ~ ~ ~ ~ ~ ~ ~

The crowd is, um, familiar. At least a few dozen of them, I believe, had trampled Ben's and my own front lawn just a day earlier, and the thing is, I never have had what you'd call a photographic memory. But let's put it this way:

Q: How many very large blaze-redheaded teenage girls wear bright yellow cropped pants and a tank top, with tummy (lots of it) showing?

A: Not too many.

and

Q: How many of them are carrying a sign that reads: "HOW DO YOU SLEEP AT NIGHT, AUNT TINK?"

A: Well, not too many, and not too badly at this point, actually, thanks to my new back doctor and his herbal remedies.

I look back at Miss Yellow's clothes. Have a little dignity, people.

Anyway, the thing I noticed about the crowd today was that there are actually a lot of signs of *support*.

"COME BACK TO US, AUNT TINK!" and "WE PROMISE—WILL TAKE ADVICE!" A teenage couple holds a sign reading "WILL WAIT 'TIL WE'RE MARRIED TO DO IT!" Please, people—once again, have a little dignity. But OK. Good sentiment. Although I don't really remember ever telling anyone not to have sex. And I think I would remember such a thing. But people read what they want to into things all the time.

Having seen enough, I move away from the window. Sister Diana and Sister Howard are both next to me.

"Go out and talk to them, for God's sake, Diana," says Sister Howard. "Lead them in a prayer or something. You never know when the Holy Spirit might send us a convert or two. After all, Tink came here for our advice."

And she puts her arm around my shoulder and leads me to a quieter place in the next room.

She looks at me.

"It looks like your 'people' want you back."

"Yeah," I answer, not feeling all that spiffy about it. I mean, in a way, it was easier when I could run away and escape and not have to worry about anything. Teacups and blogs behind me, I at least had a chance to start getting in touch with the rich sadness of missing my mom, and with the tender love I have for Ben.

"Where do I go from here?" I ask Sister Howard. "I don't even know why they'd want me back. I was barely doing a *half*-uh, you know—*assed*—job of things, even on a good day."

We sit for a minute.

"Look. You have to figure out what really makes you sing. Then do it. And take care of yourself in the process," she says.

In the distance, the crowd is now nearly silent.

I take a few more minutes with her in what we call "quiet reflection" here at the convent. I know, I never thought I'd use that expression either. I hate it when that happens.

{CHAPTER 56}

In a strange and ridiculous turn of events, Katrinka is able to wend her way to, once again, taking control of her life.

And so, our job as careful observer ends, as our hero shows her emerging true princess colors…

I head outside. Sister Diana now has the crowd humming "Amazing Grace" and holding hands. OK, I made that part up. But at least people have stopped shoving each other to reach the ice-cream truck that has pulled up at the sidewalk next to the convent.

I look around, and it's—OH. MY. GOD. It's so much clearer now what is going on. I mean, it's like the surprise birthday party I've been asking for! Mixed in with a bunch of people I can only assume are some of my readers, or possibly just curious passersby, are many of my family members! ALI and her husband JOHN and my wonderful GRANDCHILDREN are here. (*Oh, no. I forgot about our vacation this coming week on the coast.*) LITTLE TINK is here from New York City. And DYLAN. He's holding a sign that reads "Mom! Can you help me get the guest room ready for my girlfriend?" And my brother RICHARD. He has a sign that reads "Have TICKET for CONCERT tonight—Will buy DRINKS afterward! INQUIRE HERE!"

STOP. EVERYTHING.

Who is that familiar-looking woman walking around in the perimeter, strumming a guitar? Why, the nerve! It's that *JORDAN* person. How dare—? Wait a minute, wait a minute…she's waving to someone. I follow her look. Over to the other side. Smiling now… huh?…Oh. Oh. Oh! She and *Richard* (!) are giving each other these big smiles and now he's motioning to her to come join him. Wow. They look *very* happy to see each other. She looks…nice.

Hm-m-m…maybe *indirect* matchmaking is the way to go.

I continue to scan the crowd. There's my cousin LORRAINE. She is looking fabulous in her new chic Oscar de la Renta outfit, and a nun she ain't—I mean, consider her cleavage! And next to her is my sweet friend ADELINE. She looks like she knew this would happen all along. And FATHER ROB. He is smiling and waving to me in his kind and understated way and mouthing something…something…huh?…oh!…*You owe me breakfast*! Oh, yeah, I still owe him breakfast. And there are a few scattered friends and coworkers and a young couple, the male holding a sign "It's me! GARY!!" (*HOLY SHIT! GARY*?!? Wow. Really geeky looking, but kind of, well, cute. Like a young Clark Kent/ Superman.) With a darling young woman I assume is the girlfriend. And believe me, they look like they made up. And huh? DR. D. is here. Probably needs me to spoon-feed him his cereal. At least he doesn't look like he's about to take a crap or have a nervous breakdown anymore. But if I stay at the convent and don't return to work again, well, it will be pretty hard for him. And my DAD! Someone has brought him here and he's in his wheelchair, of course, looking amused and has no clue as to what's going on and just looking as happy as all get-out.

I am overwhelmed.

And then, through the crowd, I see someone emerging.

Ben.

On a white horse.

Oh, please. You didn't *really* think…

Actually, Ben *is* here. He's the one pushing Dad's wheelchair. You gotta love a man who would bring an old man along to persuade his fiancée to rejoin the world, in all its craziness.

He leaves my dad for a minute and comes over to me.

"Where's the chocolate mousse mocha cake?" I ask, giggling like a four-year-old.

"It's not your birthday for another month," he reminds me and gives me a hug. And a kiss. A really good one. With a few nuns standing right there. Even Sister Howard is all misty-eyed.

THE BIG WRAP-UP, THANK GOD!!!

That night, before bed, I set the alarm for 3 a.m. It's mean, but I can't help myself. When it goes off, tired as I am, I pick up the phone and dial.

A moment later, a groggy and somewhat distressed Dr. Myers calls back.

I take a deep breath and try to keep a smile from emerging.

"Hi, Dr. Myers. It's Tink. I almost forgot to wish you good luck on the State inspection tomorrow!"

{(THE VERY) LAST WORD}

"Tink?

Can you come to bed now, sweetie?"

Ben is at the top of the stairs, looking into the office at me, a hopeful look in his eyes.

Oh, poor Ben. He's been so patient with me.

I mean, after the big convent rally, he re-proposed to me, and I told him OK but I insisted that we get married at the convent in the beautiful gardens. He loved that and actually volunteered to return to do some work on their gardens over the summer. Even though he's not Catholic.

~ ~ ~ ~ ~ ~ ~ ~

We got married a few weeks later and the nuns sang "Climb Every Mountain" just like I always dreamed of. They even wore their "dress" habits (white!) and Ali helped get them just sparkling. She was happy to stay in Maine for a while after our vacation, which turned out to be a great one for all of us. Fr. Rob came back to do the vows and excused Ben from the religious difference as long as "you bring the children up Catholic!" Well, we're pretty old and tired to start setting a world's record, even though, of course, my gynecologist was wrong and I did not stop my period just because I turned the magic age of 55. So much for that wisdom.

Dylan, home for the summer, helped take care of his Hipa during our wedding ceremony and volunteered to be "on call" for special problems while we went away for a few days. I briefed him on the fine points of hiding the nail clippers before we left.

Richard dated Jordan for a few weeks, but stopped because she was more of a flake than he could take, but not before they made some music together.

Little Tink stayed with us for those first few weeks, having gotten very tired of the traveling tours and constant auditions, and ended up renting a tiny space a few blocks away and opening a bake shop that specialized in tea and "healthy" cookies. It worked so well and so fast that she decided to expand and ended up with four shops. Several weeks later, business booming, she was offered a movie role in L.A. (Some bigwig picked her up off my blog.) She promptly locked the doors to her shops and booked a flight west. The Sisters later took over the tea and cookie shops as a way to raise money for charitable causes. I go there now and then and treat myself to a little caffeinated tea and I don't think my breasts have even noticed.

I resumed my blog, but not before I hired a computer specialist I know. Turns out *Gary* showed me how to do things right so I could send the nasty e-mails off to the appropriate places. I realized he was only slightly weird, and actually a sweetheart of a guy. He and his girlfriend stayed together. They live in the next town. Just because someone chats with you on a blog, I discovered, doesn't mean they're a thousand miles away.

Lorraine got hired as a consultant on a project in Chicago for the renovation of a large art gallery. She flies out there once a month for a few days, leaving her little time to think about teacups.

A couple of weeks after I restarted the blog, I got an offer to go on *Ellen*. Her talk show manager wanted to bill me as "an advice columnist who's not afraid to speak the truth!" I politely declined, as "I just…well, I just want a little peace, a little R & R." I tried to say it sweetly (you know, hormones) but it may have come out something like:

"CAN'T EVERYBODY JUST LEAVE ME THE HELL ALONE FOR A FEW MINUTES?!?!?"

At least some of the time, I still try to sugarcoat things. I mean, if I spoke the truth, I'd be in deep shit, like, all the time.

Ben happily opened a charge account at the big-box hardware store and installed a third, then a fourth mailbox.

I bought Ben a beautiful, big new tent for his last birthday, along with instructions on how to keep the camping experience wonderful for us both. He had trouble figuring out the part about booking a hotel. But you know, most hotel rooms are large enough for a decent-sized tent to fit in.

The End.

Acknowledgments

This darned book took me about a hundred years to finish and get published, mostly because there were a lot of fun social media posts to read, I needed to find out what color my soul is and how many movie themes from the '70s I could remember, and I had to secretly check up on my grown kids, because it had been at least an hour since I'd heard from them. And then there were all the *Archie* comics I had to catch up on.

OK. Hang on. I believe I am now having a true moment of gratitude.

There are so many people who helped me get my novel completed and published.

I wish to express my heartfelt appreciation to:

~ God. I mean it. God really is great.

~ My late husband, Ted, without whom I would have chucked the manuscript and computer right out the window, again and again. And that would have gotten pretty expensive and taken funds away from necessities, like really good cake and weight-loss books. Ted read my manuscript even though it's chick lit. He encouraged me, let me ignore him when I was working on it, and gave me his studied nod of approval, with tears in his eyes: "It's good." Then again, he did that when he looked over the grocery list. I love you, Ted.

~ *Beyond thanks* to my friend and cartoonist Bill Eldridge, who poured heart, soul, and pen into what only meager words could express. The poor guy got quite accustomed to hearing, "Oh…I should have told you that what I *really* meant was…." He deserves a medal.

~ My mother Marge, who took me under her writing wing (I believe it was her right side) before she had the nerve to pack up and move to Heaven. Thanks, Mom, for teaching me to laugh at life.

~ *Maine Women* magazine editor and friend Jane Lord, who called me one day in 2009 and asked me if I'd like to write a column. Thank you, Jane, for teaching me so many things about editing, including not using too many exclamation points!!!! That is, like, SO important!!!!!!!!!! Also, thank you for introducing me and my hips to that fabulous gourmet ice cream place near the office. I'll meet you there in half an hour.

~ My family, particularly my children Cassie, Sally, and William—and other relations, who patiently read my stuff over the years, gave me feedback (which was better than giving me lip), and even helped with title ideas. Thank you, Cassie, for being my go-to person for reading, editing, and more, including making me the best chocolate chip cookies ever. Other readers include my nieces Lili, Kathy, and Lula, who read all or part of the manuscript.

~ My cousin Fred and his wife Meryl (my BBFF) and my sister Laurie, all of whom dove into the title discussion with relish. And artichokes.

~ My friend Denise (BFF) who read my manuscript, didn't criticize my use of foul language, and helped with the tidal wave of title discussions; and my friends Kathy and John, for also entitling me to discuss the title.

~ My writing friends Cathy Turney, Jerry Zezima, Suzette Standring, Bridie Clark, Shonna Milliken Humphrey, Dave Astor, Jane Lord, and Lyn McCafferty for support, advice, cheerleading, expertise, critiques… the list of their generosity of spirit and talent goes on and on.

~ My thanks to Rick Wolff, for his helpful publishing advice and willingness to share his expertise and talent.

~ My family and friends: You are my inspiration. If you happen to recognize a character who bears a slight resemblance to you or someone you know, please don't sue me. All you would get would be a big pile of books called *Not Even Dark Chocolate Can Fix This Mess* and a half-eaten chocolate bar. (Make that three-quarters eaten.)

~ My son-in-law Paul, who made pancakes for me in my last frenzied days of book decisions.

~ Julianna Stoll, my BBFF Meryl's daughter, who designed my original blog, is my web designer, and who, FYI, is just adorable.

~ Joshua Bodwell, director of Maine Writers and Publishers Alliance (MWPA), for his lovely help and support.

~ My friends at MWPA and the National Society of Newspaper Columnists (NSNC) who have so kindly encouraged my efforts. TYVM.

~ Genie Dailey, my sharp and wonderful editor at Maine Authors Publishing, and the entire amazing staff of MAP: Jane Karker, Nikki Giglia, Cheryl McKeary, Dan Karker, Lindy Gifford, Morgen Benz, and genius graphic designer David Allen. Without you, my dream would have been simply that. You brought my book to life. Thank you.

~ My Facebook friends, some cyber-friends, some Rye Neck High School classmates, some friends of friends, some unfriends…your encouragement and love have made all the difference. You know who you are. I love you. Write your name here: _____.

~ And finally, many people who have truly inspired me and led to composite characters and situations of my imagination: my family; my very beloved Sisters of Mercy and Mercy Associates; Fr. Fred Nickle; my brother Steve; my Dutch relatives and friends; my dear departed dad Larry; my friend Jeri; various coworkers, hairdressers, food servers past and present; my sweet dog Rebel who is in Doggy Heaven; in-laws and step-persons who have excused me from moments of family participation because "I have a deadline! Now where's that chocolate bar I hid somewhere?!? GET IT!!!"

~ My local Starbucks peeps, who have served me lovely beverages and allowed me to sit working for hours on end in the pleasant bustle of their cozy café. I love you guys.

~ And did I mention God? Thank you, God.